SURE FOOTING
IN A
SHAKY
WORLD

A Woman's Journey To Security

by Kathy Collard Miller

Aglow Publications

A Ministry of Women's Aglow Fellowship, Int'l.
P.O. Box 1548
Lynnwood, WA 98046-1558
USA

Cover design by Ray Braun

ISBN 0-932305-60-1

To
six important women in my life,
in whom I've seen security blossom:
My mother, Vivian
My mother-in-law, Audrey
My sister, Karen
My cousin, Dorie
My sister-in-law, Leslie
and last but not least, my daughter, Darcy

Acknowledgements

I'm grateful to Gloria Chisholm, my editor, for challenging me to make this a stronger and deeper book. Her insights were valuable and creative. Thank you, Gloria!

Contents

Introduction

My neighbor, Pat LaGraffe, and I took our children and three of their friends to nearby Disneyland for the day. As we waited for the Captain EO theater doors to open, a woman walked through the crowd holding her three-year-old son. Folded over the crook of her arm and held by the boy was the most threadbare baby blanket I've ever seen. Large holes allowed the little boy to wind his fingers through it.

"There's a well-used blanket," I whispered to Pat. "Mark's blanket almost got that bad."

As we stared at the amusing scene, I thought, *Each of us has our own security blankets we depend on, often replacing the security we could find in the Lord.*

What kind of security am I talking about? Bill Gothard's 1989 Calendar defines it as "Building my life around what is eternal and cannot be destroyed or taken away."

Doesn't that sound wonderful? Yet I sometimes find more security in my ability to manipulate life the way I want it to be, rather than depending on God's ability to fulfill his plan for my life. At other times, as a way of growing secure, I try to force people to change instead of waiting for God to make the transformations he wants.

All of us, to one degree or another, use methods other than God's way to bolster our security in the Lord. But wouldn't it be wonderful to have complete assurance of God's love even though we're not perfect? Wouldn't it be encouraging to know that our growth process is leading us to maturity? Wouldn't it be satisfying to have strength to respond to others in a godly manner? These goals are not unrealistic and helping you achieve them—to deepen your security in God—is the prime objective of this book.

In *Sure Footing in a Shaky World,* I'll share my own struggles and victories, and I trust you'll grow from the things I've learned. You'll also read about other women who have developed greater security because of their responses to the circumstances in their lives. Whether you consider yourself a secure woman, one totally lacking in security, or someone in between, this book is for you. As you implement the practical ideas you find here you, too, can achieve greater security.

I hope that reading *Sure Footing in a Shaky World* will strengthen your ability to look at life from a heavenly perspective, enabling you to deal with your earthly journey's problems in God's power.

Kathy Collard Miller
Placentia, California
April 1989

1
···

You Can Be
a Secure Woman

Kate slowly replaced the phone on its cradle and stared into space, the color draining from her face.

"Who was that, Mommy?" Ten-year-old Matt looked up from his homework scattered on the kitchen table.

"Daddy. He just lost his job."

"We won't have to move from our new house, will we?"

"I don't know." Kate moved like a robot across the kitchen and into the hall. She stumbled into the bedroom where tears cascaded down her cheeks. Walking past the dresser, she punched her fist into the wood, barely noticing the pain.

Lord, this isn't fair! We're finally getting on our feet financially, and now Garry gets laid off. We came to this town for that job. How are we going to make our house payment?

Kate felt her heart race and the room spin as she plopped on the edge of the bed. *I've got to find a job! If I don't do something, we'll go bankrupt!* She hurried out of the room intent on finding the newspaper. As she passed through the living room, she noticed her open Bible, which she'd left on the sofa after her devotions that morning. She stopped abruptly.

Wait a minute. Wait a minute! *Lord, in my panic I've forgotten that you are the great God who owns a thousand cattle on the hillside.* She sat down, picked up the Bible, and read what she had underlined that morning in 1 Chronicles 29:11: "Yours, O Lord, is the greatness and the power and the glory and the majesty and the splendor, for everything in the heaven and the earth is yours. Yours, O Lord, is the kingdom; and you are exalted as head over all."

Kate leaned back into the floral print of the sofa pillows, sucked in a deep breath, and then let it out slowly. "How can I forget so quickly, Father?" she whispered. "You haven't changed since this morning when I praised you for your powerful sovereignty. You're still in control! Maybe I will have to get a job, but I'm not going to look until Garry and I decide together. I'm not going to let circumstances tear down my faith. You'll guide us and provide a new job for Garry. Thank you!"

Kate jumped up from the couch and strode into the kitchen. Matt looked at her with fear in his eyes. He'd been crying. "Mom, are we going to have to move again?"

Wrapping her arms around Matt's shoulders, Kate kissed his hair. "Honey, I'm so sorry I frightened you. My trust in God really got knocked over for a moment, but now I'm all right. I don't know how God is going to provide for us, but I know he will. Just you wait and see."

Like Kate, we all have circumstances and people in our lives who threaten to tear down our faith and security in God. Feeling insecure, we experience panic. We want to do things our own way or try to change other people. During those times we have trouble believing God is still in control.

Naturally, we would always like to feel completely secure, but we all experience degrees of insecurity. We thirst to know without a doubt who we are in Christ. We long to experience abundant life while on earth and also be assured eternal life when we leave. We crave the confidence that enables us to exercise God's power in our positions as daughters of the King.

Our craving for security is normal. As Christian psychologist Larry Crabb notes in his book *Effective Biblical Counseling*:

> The most basic need is a sense of personal worth, an acceptance of oneself as a whole, real person. The two required inputs are *significance* (purpose, importance, adequacy for a job, meaningfulness, impact) and *security* (love—unconditional and consistently expressed; permanent acceptance). . . . My experience suggests that although men and women need both kinds of input, for men the primary route to personal worth is significance and for women the primary route is security.[1]

Crabb identifies security as knowing we are unconditionally loved, accepted, and cared for now and forever. When we are convinced of this, we can respond confidently, trustingly, lovingly, fearlessly, and realistically to life's problems and difficulties.

But in our struggle for security, God's still small voice is often drowned out by the loud clamor of other voices around us, all shouting about "real" security! Society and our spiritual enemies say, "Have it your own way. Do your own thing. Be an individual." American materialistic society tries to convince us that finding security is climbing up the corporate ladder, a Mercedes in the driveway, and a Saks dress hanging in the closet.

To the world, feeling secure is realizing that even if your husband doesn't understand you, the man at the office does. Advertisements sport the latest fashions, possessions, and accomplishments as ways to make sure you are significant and loved. TV sitcoms give the impression that security is solving family problems within thirty minutes.

As if that's not enough, New Age thinking teaches that security is believing "you are god" and that occult practices such as channeling provide the way to feel loved and important. These viewpoints differ from God's definition of security in every respect.

Daniel 11:32 tells us, "The people who know their God will display strength and take action" (NASB). In God's eyes, a secure, strong woman is someone who knows God—the true Almighty God of the universe. Larry Crabb describes her security well.

God has seen me at my worst and still loved me to the point of giving His life for me. That kind of love I can never lose. I am completely acceptable to him regardless of my behavior. I am under no pressure to earn or to keep his love. My acceptability to God depends only on Jesus' acceptability to God and on the fact that Jesus' death was counted as full payment for my sins. Now that I know this love I can relax, secure in the knowledge that the eternal God of creation has pledged to use his infinite power and wisdom to insure my welfare. That's security. Nothing can happen to me that my loving God doesn't allow. I will experience nothing he will not enable me to handle. When problems mount and I feel alone, insecure, and afraid, I am to fill my mind with the security-building truth that at this moment a sovereign, loving, personal, infinite God is absolutely in control. In this knowledge, I rest secure.[2]

The attributes of a godly, secure person are spelled out clearly in Psalm 112:

Praise the Lord.
Blessed is the man who fears the Lord, who finds great delight in his commands.
His children will be mighty in the land; each generation of the upright will be blessed.
Wealth and riches are in his house, and his righteousness endures forever.
Even in darkness light dawns for the upright, for the gracious and compassionate and righteous man.
Good will come to him who is generous and lends freely, who conducts his affairs with justice.
Surely he will never be shaken; a righteous man will be remembered forever.
He will have no fear of bad news; his heart is steadfast, trusting in the Lord.
His heart is secure, he will have no fear; in the end he will look in triumph on his foes.
He has scattered abroad his gifts to the poor, his righteousness endures forever; his horn will be lifted high in honor.

The wicked man will see and be vexed, he will gnash his teeth and waste away; the longings of the wicked will come to nothing.

This passage also shows us the security-building characteristics God desires to establish in each woman:

- She fears God and loves to study his Word.
- She is confident her future is in God's hands.
- She depends not on material prosperity for security, but on God.
- She is gracious and compassionate toward others.
- She is not easily shaken.
- She exhibits courage in the face of bad news.
- She doesn't worry because she trusts God.
- She is convinced that in the end God will be victorious in her struggles.
- She is generous to others because she knows God will provide for her needs.

The secure Christian woman focuses on Jesus, sees life from God's viewpoint, and considers failure an opportunity for growth. She is wise, yet humble, recognizing her gifts, but also acknowledging the one who has gifted her. Because she is assured that God is in control of her surrendered life, the secure Christian woman is not easily ruffled by circumstances. Her main goal is to obey and please God. At the same time, she understands she's not perfect; therefore, she will always experience some degree of insecurity. She recognizes this paradox can be positive because insecurity keeps her dependent on the Lord instead of on herself.

I long to have these qualities fulfilled in my life. I believe every woman does. Unfortunately, many Christian women do not experience this kind of security. Why? Let's look again to Larry Crabb for some possible reasons:

"My thesis is that problems develop when the basic needs for significance and security are threatened. People pursue irresponsible ways of living as a means of defending against feelings of insignificance and insecurity. In most cases these folks have arrived at a wrong idea as to what constitutes significance and security. And these false beliefs are at the core of their problems."[3]

One morning recently, I almost succumbed to a false belief when my husband Larry began dressing for work. He pulled a too-small shirt out of the dry-cleaning bag and gasped. "Oh, no, they mixed up the shirts," he exclaimed in an irritated tone. "And the missing one is my most expensive."

I cringed because I had picked up the shirts from the laundry. Why hadn't I noticed the wrong one mixed in with the others? Because I felt guilty, I wanted to shout, "Well, you don't have to blame me. It's not my fault!"

Then I realized Larry wasn't blaming me. My old insecure pattern of thinking everything was my fault had raised its ugly head again. Immediately, I corrected my wrong thinking and reminded myself that I'm not responsible for everything that happens. *It's not my fault, it's the dry cleaner's fault. I can't be expected to look through every set of laundry I pick up. It's okay, Kathy, relax.*

As a result, instead of responding angrily to Larry, I empathized with his annoyance and replied, "That's so irritating when they do that. Do you want me to check out a different laundry?"

Insecurity can rise up within us in many ways. My friend, Connie, a childhood incest victim, faces insecurity whenever she confuses love and sexual involvement. Her father's words as he molested her were, "I love you. You're a good girl." As a result, love to her was physical and often painful. Today, as a single woman, she struggles with wanting love from others and thinking she'll find it by giving in to sexual immorality.

In my correspondence file is a letter from Julia, who struggles with anger. Her insecurity involves doubting that she'll ever get control of it. She longs for God to instantaneously deliver her. But God wants to work a process of growth within her that will pull out the roots of her insecurities. Julia also feels insecure because her pastor wrongly told her that her continuing struggle could cause her to lose her salvation.

Tammy is another woman who deals with a form of insecurity—she can't say no. Because she believes it's a sign of weakness, she agrees to take on more responsibilities even though her schedule is full. She's afraid of hurting other's feelings or letting them down. As a result, she's frazzled and short-tempered, and she often wonders why she can't find time to spend with the Lord.

To some extent, I've struggled with all the above challenges. Although I'm not an incest victim like Connie, when I was a child, a boy touched me in an inappropriate place, and I blamed myself. Like Julia, I've struggled with abusive anger and for a time thought God couldn't possibly deliver me from it. I even wondered if he still loved me. And similar to Tammy, I've had a hard time learning to say no. So I understand these insecurities—but I've also seen the Lord develop greater security in me. I know he can do the same for you.

Remember Kate from the beginning of this chapter? Even though she felt overwhelmed by the loss of Garry's job and experienced feelings of insecurity, she decided to exercise her faith, trust God, and remain secure.

Today, Kate's circumstances are still less than "secure" in themselves. Garry has a temporary job, and the Lord has provided a part-time job for Kate that works in well with the children's school hours. However, they may still have to sell their home to buy one with lower payments. Kate's emotions fluctuate continually, but her faith is growing as is her sense of security.

Would you like to experience more security in the midst of your challenging life? It's possible. Come along with me as we discover how to become the secure and confident women God wants us to be.

2
...

A Secure Woman Prays with Boldness

Mark came home from the third day of sixth grade near tears. "What happened, honey?" I asked.

"Oh, nothing." He looked away in embarrassment.

"I know you're sad about something. Please tell me."

He fiddled with the zipper on his backpack. A few moments passed while he pulled out his notebook, then he said weakly, "Matt and David teased me at lunch today. Yesterday they threw food at me. Can't you take me out of school for lunchtime tomorrow?"

"I can sure understand that you don't want to be there if they're teasing you, but I can't do it tomorrow. How about the next day?"

Mark tossed his notebook on the table. "No, it has to be tomorrow," he fumed.

21

"Can't you ignore them or sit somewhere else?"

"No, we sit at assigned tables. They're at the table next to me. Even if I ignore them, they make fun of me."

"Mark, I really think we need to tell the teacher about this."

"No, no, don't do that." He looked up at me with fear-filled eyes. "That'll just give them more things to tease me about."

I could see his logic but replied, "The teacher could watch and take care of it. They'd never know we told her."

"But they mimic me without being obvious. No one else can tell what they're doing."

I didn't know what else to say. Mark saw no hope of anything changing.

"Well, honey, we'll just have to pray and ask God to help you."

Doubt crossed Mark's face. How could God help him? I wasn't sure, either, but Mark needed help, and I couldn't be at school to protect him.

The next morning as Mark walked out the door, I said, "Honey, Daddy and I prayed for you last night, and I'm going to call a friend this morning to pray, too. Don't worry, you're going to see a difference."

Moments later, I called Patsy. As I filled her in on the details, I began to cry. "Patsy, I feel so sorry for him. He feels so alone, and he can't see how God can help him. I feel helpless, too, but I just know that if we pray, God will do something."

My mind flashed through several scenarios of how God might work. Matt and David would walk up to Mark and apologize. Or as they teased him, Mark would look straight at them, and say, "God loves you and so do I." Or maybe another friend would say, "Mark's my friend, don't tease him." I knew my ideas were unrealistic, but I wanted so much to see some dramatic display of God's power.

I also realized that God often works in more subtle ways and, as Patsy prayed, I felt strengthened. After I hung up, I left my concern for Mark with the Lord and went about my day without worry.

When Mark returned home from school that afternoon, he found me waiting eagerly near the door. He tossed his backpack on the kitchen counter. "How was lunchtime, Mark?" I quickly asked.

"Oh, fine," he replied without expression.

"Well, did Matt and David bug you?"

"No."

"Did you do anything different?"

"I just sat as far away from them as I could."

"Good for you. I think the Lord helped you do something about your problem. Can you see that?"

"Uh, maybe."

Mark's faith was still too weak to recognize God's hand working in a quiet way. But I praised God regardless, because the day hadn't been traumatic for my son.

Mark went off to school each day after that a little more confident in his ability to handle lunchtime. Several weeks have passed, and he hasn't said any more about being teased. A few days ago, Matt suddenly showed up at our door, and he and Mark played together for the afternoon.

My trust in God helped me resist an insecure reaction during that mini-crisis. If I had relied upon my own resources instead of prayer, I might have told Mark to react meanly to the boys (it did cross my mind). Or I might have called them and asked them to stop teasing Mark (Mark would have been even more embarrassed by that). But because I allowed God to lead me, I felt secure and could wait to see his solution.

At times, God's solution is that we take action; we can

also be secure then. But in handling any problem, let's first pray. Our loving heavenly Father is even more concerned about our lives than we are.

How does prayer make us more secure? If being secure means we feel loved by God and, as a result, we can confidently face life's pressures and problems, how is prayer a vehicle for accomplishing this? Here are some points to consider.

I AM NOT HELPLESS

Have you ever had a concern and no one to turn to? Before I knew the Lord, I carried a continual heaviness in my heart because I had no place to take my anxieties. Would I choose the right major in college? Would I marry the right person? Why couldn't I be happy all the time? What happened after death?

Although I considered myself a Christian, I didn't have the inner assurance that God loved me. I wondered if God really wanted to involve himself in my life. I strove to be "good enough" to earn his love and acceptance—along with his help for my problems.

I no longer face life this way. Now I remind myself that Jesus said, "Come to me, all you who are weary and burdened, and I will give you rest" (Matt. 11:28). Or "The Lord will accomplish what concerns me" (Ps. 138:8 NASB).

T.B. Matson says, "Prayer is not something to be added after other approaches in our search for the will of God have been tried and have failed. No, we should pray as we use the personal resources God has given us."[1]

When seemingly uncontrollable circumstances face a woman, she can choose to pray and increase her security. She isn't helpless.

GOD PROMISES TO RESPOND

Not only does the secure woman have somewhere to take her burdens, but she is assured that God will respond. He promises in John 15:7, "If you abide in Me, and My words abide in you, ask whatever you wish, and it shall be done for you" (NASB). Her confidence is based also on God's pledge that his plan will be accomplished, although she accepts the possibility that he may not always answer in exactly the way she wants.

When I hear people say, "God answered my prayer!" I usually assume they mean, "He responded in the way I asked him to." This doesn't always happen. God answers our prayers in one of three ways: yes, no, or wait.

He doesn't always answer our petitions with an immediate yes. When Matt and David were teasing Mark, I wanted the answer "yes" to include the boys' apologizing to Mark. Then I realized this was a little farfetched, and I asked God to work however he wanted to. I would have preferred a dramatic display of his power, but he didn't choose to act in this way. He answered in his own way.

If the situation we've prayed about doesn't change, can we as secure women still believe God has heard our prayers? Yes, because his answer may be "wait." Or maybe he's moving in ways we can't see yet. Regardless, we can remain confident he is working. Deuteronomy 33:12 says, "Let the beloved of the Lord rest secure in him, for he shields him all day long, and the one the Lord loves rests between his shoulders."

Not only will God answer my prayers, but he'll guide me in the way he wants me to take. What security! No longer must I wonder which route is right. This doesn't mean I will always be certain what to do or never do the wrong thing, but as I learn to recognize the Holy Spirit's voice within me, I will experience increased success in knowing his will.

The secure woman can face anything because she knows God will lead her. At times, Satan may whisper, "What will you do if your husband has an affair?" "What will you do if your children take drugs?" "What will you do if Linda gossips about you?" When we're secure, we can be assured that if any of these things happen, God will guide us at the time. We don't need to worry about them now, but we can make godly choices to help prevent these things from occurring.

If we are convinced that God will act in response to our prayers, our security level will increase.

GOD WILL DO WHAT'S RIGHT

Insecurity arises out of fear that what *we* think is the best solution to a problem, won't be the one *God* chooses. We may feel an overwhelming desire to manipulate circumstances to happen the way we believe they should.

The secure woman leaves the results to God, confident that he is the blessed controller of all things and gives only good gifts to his children. Although he may not always work exactly the way she'd like, she trusts his wisdom to do the best thing. As she prays, she can say, "Lord, you know what I'd like to see happen, and I ask for that if it's your will. But if in your great knowledge you want something better, I ask you to do that instead."

Psalm 16:5 assures her, "Lord, you have assigned me my portion and my cup; you have made my lot secure." With David, she can feel secure because whatever God allows is for her best. This doesn't mean, for example, that if she has an illness, she doesn't take appropriate measures, or she never takes action to solve her problems. But it does mean she trusts God to work for her best whatever circumstances she faces.

Augustus Strong writes, "God can do all He will, but He will not do all He can. Else His power is mere force acting necessarily, and God (would be) the slave of His own omnipotence. God is not compelled to do all He can do, but uses as much of His power as He pleases. Just because He is omnipotent, He does not have to do all He can do."[2]

Evelyn Christenson, author of *What Happens When Women Pray,* tells about the time her friend, Elmy, took over the responsibility of the prayer chain.

When Elmy took over I said to her, "You're going to have a problem. Some people will be calling to give you *answers* instead of requests. When they ask you to pray that such and such will happen, tell them kindly, "We do not pray answers, we pray requests."

Do you see the difference? When we pray answers, we're demanding that God do something and telling Him we want it done now. . . . When we're bringing our requests to Him, we're saying, "Lord, here's the need" . . . then we ask Him to answer according to His omniscient will.[3]

We can leave the results with God. That doesn't mean we can't make suggestions, but if we are secure, ultimately, we will want what God wants, not what we want.

PRAYER MAKES GOD'S POWER AVAILABLE

The helpless, fearful woman can mature into a secure woman when she realizes God's incredible power is accessible to her. Paul said, "I pray also that the eyes of your heart may be enlightened in order that you may know the hope to which he has called you, the riches of his glorious inheritance in the saints, and his incomparably great power for us who believe" (Eph. 1:18, 19).

This power helps her change wrong attitudes. God's power convicts people when they seem completely selfish. This power performs miraculous healing in body and spirit even when it seems impossible. Hope becomes the secure woman's strength because she believes God's power through prayer can make a difference. "You will be secure, because there is hope; you will look about you and take your rest in safety" (Job 11:18).

According to Ray Stedman in *Spiritual Warfare*, "Our prayers play a direct and essential part in bringing God's invisible power to bear on visible life. In other words, God answers prayer."[4]

Evelyn Christenson writes,

Recently, an occult high priest was quoted in our local newspaper. He said that the churches of America had given up the supernatural. They don't deal in the supernatural; they just deal in plans and programs and social action. He said that every human being is created with a supernatural vacuum, and since Christians aren't doing anything in the realm of the supernatural, he feels that witchcraft is a reasonable substitute for Christianity.[5]

Those of us who are growing more secure *are* taking hold of God's supernatural power through prayer. Jeanne did this recently when she confronted her father about his sin of incest toward her many years earlier. "I never could have done that even three months ago," she said. "But with God's and my counselor's help, and lots of prayer, God gave me the strength to face my father with the truth. He still denies it and that hurts me deeply, but I know that

28

God will continue to restore my emotional being."

The secure woman has power as she claims it in prayer.

PRAYER GIVES ME AUTHORITY

As daughters of our heavenly Father, we have every spiritual blessing available to us. Through prayer, we can avail ourselves of those privileges. We receive forgiveness of sin, freedom from worry, boldness to enter his presence, redemption from the eternal power of sin, joy in spite of difficulties, contentment regardless of disappointments, and an identity with purpose.

The insecure woman is like an orphan who is asked, "Who are your parents, and where do you come from?" Because the orphan has no identity to name, she feels abandoned and unloved.

But the secure woman knows her spiritual roots and heritage. She can confidently reply to Satan, "I am the daughter of Almighty God, who defeated you through his Son at Calvary. I have all the powers of God at my disposal, and I'm protected by God's hand. You can't hurt or influence me without first going through the filter of God's love. I'm secure in him."

The paradox of this authority is that it also puts us in a position of humility, for we become completely dependent upon God. Catherine Marshall says,

A little child who has no shyness or hesitation about asking his parents for what he needs is unselfconsciously revealing his helplessness—along with a normal, right relationship with his father and mother. In the same way, asking immediately puts us into a right relationship with God. It is acting out the fact that He is the creator with the riches and resources we need; we are the creatures who need help. It's a cap-in-hand stance which we resist because it diminishes us—a certain amount of pride and self has to go for us to ask for help—whether of God or of another human being.[6]

Through that dependence upon God, we have a Father/daughter relationship with the Almighty God of the universe. Prayer is the key that brings me into his inner chamber at his palace to claim my position as princess.

I HAVE INTIMACY WITH GOD

During times of prayer, we focus on God's qualities and thus know him better. Such knowledge swells our faith because we realize more and more that our security is based on a loving, dependable, compassionate God who can never fail or sin.

Several years ago, as I began focusing on one attribute of God each day during my daily prayer time, my security grew immensely.

I'm careful to distinguish this praise time as different from my "thanking" time. Praise is when we focus on *who* God is; thanking God concentrates on *what* He does. For instance, when I felt so bad about Mark's being teased at school, I praised God for his love. I said something like, "Lord, you are a loving God. Your love is so great that you love Mark far more than I do. Your love wants only the best for him. I praise you for your wonderful, complete love."

After I praised him, I continued by thanking him for wanting to work in my problems. "Father, thank you that your love motivates you to protect Mark and give him courage to go to school and face whatever he must. Thank you for working in this situation so that Mark's faith can grow as he sees you intervene. I'm so grateful, Lord. I love you all the more."

Whenever you feel overwhelmed and tempted to think like an insecure woman, focus your mind on who God is.

Do you feel fearful? Concentrate on God's power.

Do you feel unappreciated? Focus on God's love.

Do you feel overwhelmed? Think about God's sufficiency.

Do you view yourself as foolish? Meditate on his wisdom.

Do you experience depression? Dwell on his joyfulness.

Do you sense rejection from others? Consider his complete acceptance.

Through prayer, the secure woman becomes better acquainted with her wonderful, heavenly Father.

I HAVE BOLD ACCESS TO GOD

Ephesians 3:11, 12 assures us, "This was in accordance with the eternal purpose which He carried out in Christ Jesus our Lord, in whom we have boldness and confident access through faith in Him" (NASB).

Imagine for a moment that you have a difficult problem, and you're convinced that speaking to the president of the United States will solve it.

"He has the authority I need to take care of this problem," you tell yourself. "I'll go to Washington, D.C. and talk to him." But then the doubts begin. "I'm an insignificant person. Even though I'm a citizen, the president doesn't care about little ol' me. I'd be a fool to try to talk to him."

You continue to try to solve your problem but are frustrated at every turn. At the back of your mind a little voice keeps saying, "Go talk to the president. He'll help you." But you fight against such a preposterous idea.

Your problem intensifies and finally you conclude, "I

can't do anything. I must talk to the president. He's my only hope."

With great fear, you travel to Washington, D.C. Once there, you walk up to the outer gate of the White House. There stands an impressive military man in full uniform, looking stern and uncaring. Certainly, he won't let you in. "I might as well go home," you tell yourself. "No, I have no choice. I have to try."

You walk up to the guard. Gathering all your courage, you say with false boldness, "I'm a citizen of the United States, and I need to talk to the president."

Instead of laughing at you, the guard says, "If you're a citizen, of course you may see the president. Go right in." He smiles and flings the gate open for you.

Is it a joke? You walk forward, bracing your body for the gate to slam shut in your face. But it doesn't, and you keep walking.

As you approach the White House, you feel jittery and in a state of shock. You make your way to the steps and meet more guards, but they, too, open the doors for you. Stepping into the foyer, you face a receptionist, sitting behind a large oak desk. With an assurance you don't feel, you say, "I'm a citizen of the United States, and I need to talk to the president about—" Before you finish, the receptionist rises from her seat and says, "Follow me, I'll lead you to the president's office."

In awe, you walk with her through the splendor of the inner White House. After several minutes you arrive at two huge doors. She opens the right one and says, "The president will see you now."

Your mouth drops open. "Already? Don't I have to wait for an appointment? Don't you have to make sure he's available?"

"Oh, no," the receptionist replies. "He's always ready

to talk to his citizens. Go right in."

She swings open the door, and you stare into a magnificent office. Sitting at a massive desk is the man you recognize as the president of the United States. Hesitantly, you walk forward and begin awkwardly, "I didn't mean to barge in, but the receptionist said I could."

"Yes, that's right. You don't need an appointment here. Sit down. Would you like a cup of coffee or glass of iced tea?"

"Oh, no, thank you. I just want to talk about my problem. I won't keep you long. You see—even though I've read your book and tried to follow your principles, I haven't been very successful, so I really don't deserve anything."

"That's nonsense, friend. You belong here because you're a citizen of the United States. There's nothing more you can do to earn my acceptance. You have it unconditionally already. Sit down and take all the time you need."

You find yourself relaxing and sit down and sip the delicious tea he offers. You find your voice again and say, "I don't want to keep you too long, when is your next appointment?"

With a smile, he replies, "Whenever we're done. You have my undivided attention for as long as you'd like. Relax now and tell me what's on your heart."

With relief you pour out your concerns, problems, and joys. He listens attentively, often interjecting wise counsel or reflecting your feelings back to you. After some time, you both come to a decision on what to do about your problem. Now you know you'll see progress.

Suddenly, you realize that no telephone has interrupted your conversation nor has anyone come into the room to distract this important man's attention. Taking a deep breath and exhaling it, you realize you feel carefree and confident. *Why did I feel so fearful and hesitant about coming?* you wonder. *I must come back again soon, even when I don't have a problem.*

By now you know that I'm describing the access we have to our heavenly Father. No, you can't walk into the office of the president of the United States, but you can walk into the inner chamber of the Almighty God of the universe any time you wish. As a daughter-citizen of his heavenly realm, you have the right to come boldly into his presence. As long as you wear Jesus' robe of righteousness, you are fully qualified to stand before a God who is perfectly holy. No one can block your way—you have a standing appointment any time. No telephone call will steal his undivided attention from you and your concerns. No secretary will interrupt to say someone else is waiting.

While in his presence, you know you are completely accepted and loved. Even though God may sometimes gently remind you of areas in your life that need his cleansing and help, he will speak of his ability to help you. You feel relaxed and confident, knowing he has full authority and power to strengthen you to deal with your problem. You feel secure!

Make a choice to take your problems to the Lord immediately and ask for wisdom and guidance. When you do, you've made a decision to strengthen the security in your life.

3
...

A Secure Woman Stands Strong Despite Problems

One day when I was an insecure high school freshman, Chris, one of the cheerleaders, caught up with me as I headed for my locker. "Kathy, what happened in Spanish class yesterday? I was at cheerleader practice."

I stared at her in confusion—*Chris, one of the most popular girls in school, is talking to me. Me, Miss Nobody.* My heart beat wildly, and my mouth felt as dry as if I'd been eating cardboard. *I better say something fast, so I don't blow this chance.*

I swallowed and blurted out, "Oh, you didn't miss much. We practiced conversation number three. You should've seen Jeremy try to say some of the words. It was hilarious, and the whole class was laughing at him and then Mr. Hurley. . . ." I continued on and on, thrilled to have Chris' attention.

After several minutes, I noticed Chris' facial expression change from interest to boredom. She looked past me to the kids walking by. Panicked, I thought, *Oh, no, I've lost her. Kathy, you've blown it again.* My face turned beet red.

In mid-sentence, I shut my mouth and stared at her. My heart sank to shoe level, and my crystal clear visions of popularity dissolved before my eyes.

Chris smiled weakly. "Well, thanks. See ya." Turning on her heel, she joined her friends. I saw her whisper something, and then they looked back at me, laughing. I wanted to melt into the concrete slab.

She's telling everyone how stupid I am, I reasoned. *It's just a matter of time before every kid in school hears about it.*

For the next few days, as I recalled that scene over and over again, my insecurities deepened to a new low.

As a teenager, I had many problems, including low self-esteem. At the time, I thought I was the only one who had an inferiority complex. Now, of course, I know that while everyone may not suffer from low esteem, everyone has problems. These "challenges" can include a wayward child, an insensitive husband, a gossiping friend, a divided church, or a controlling mother-in-law. The list is endless.

When problems seem to suffocate us, it's easy to react with insecurity. We imagine the problems are bigger than they really are, and we doubt God can solve them. We think they will last forever. In our panic, we attempt to solve them in our own power instead of with God's strength.

Dr. M. Scott Peck, in his book *The Road Less Traveled,* identifies other reactions of the insecure woman.

Fearing the pain involved, almost all of us, to a greater or lesser degree, attempt to avoid problems. We procrastinate, hoping that they will go away. We ignore them, forget them, pretend they do not exist. We even take drugs to assist us in ignoring them, so that by deadening ourselves to the pain we can forget the problems that cause the pain. We attempt to skirt around problems rather than meet them head on. We attempt to get out of them rather than suffer through them.[1]

We don't have to react like insecure women. We've already identified the first thing a secure woman does when faced with a problem: she prays. Now let's continue our search of how she can stand strong in the Lord when faced with problems.

A SECURE WOMAN'S ATTITUDE
TOWARD PROBLEMS

Some years ago when I was bound by the chains of abusive anger towards my then-two-year-old daughter, I truly believed I was the only Christian who had ever reacted in such a sinful way. Satan used that belief to make me even more insecure and fearful of telling anyone. *I can't tell anyone about this*, I reasoned. *They could never understand. My friends don't get angry at their kids like I do.*

After God delivered me and I started speaking about my previous struggle, I was surprised when one woman told me that she, too, had abused her child, and added, "I've never told anyone this before. I thought I was the only one until I heard you share."

The Bible tells us, *"No temptation has seized you except what is common to man. And God is faithful; he will not let you be tempted beyond what you can bear. But when*

37

you are tempted, he will also provide a way out so you can stand up under it" (1 Cor. 10:13, italics added).

Not only has someone else experienced a similar problem, but Jesus has, too. "For we do not have a high priest who is unable to sympathize with our weaknesses, but we have one who has been tempted in every way, just as we are—yet was without sin" (Heb. 4:15).

Now obviously, although he was rejected, lied about, abused, and so much more, Jesus didn't experience every problem women have. Where he "sympathizes with our weaknesses" was in his internal responses to his circumstances while on earth. He understands.

The next time you feel insecure because it seems you're the only one with a particular problem, take heart. Just as Jesus overcame his temptations, many have coped victoriously. In God's power, so can you.

Problems are ever-present, but most are temporary. My former neighbor, Pam, once told me, "As soon as I take care of the problems I have right now, I can really live." That is how an insecure woman thinks. The truth is we will always have problems. Our goal is not to eliminate them, but to trust God in the midst of them.

At the same time we view problems as ever-present, we can view many of them as temporary. It is true that as soon as we solve one, another comes along; yet that one probably won't haunt us forever, either; it, too, will be solved.

Once in a testimony meeting, a Christian got up and said that the words "and it came to pass" always blessed her.

"When I am upset by troubles, I go to the Bible, and I never get far before I read 'It came to pass.' And I say 'Bless the Lord it didn't come to stay—it came to pass!' "[2]

The next time a problem seems permanent, remind yourself it most likely "came to pass." It, too, will be replaced by another, and God will use them all.

Problems are insignificant compared to heaven's glory.
"Therefore we do not lose heart. Though outwardly we are wasting away, yet inwardly we are being renewed day by day. For our light and momentary troubles have achieved for us an eternal glory that far outweighs them all" (2 Cor. 4:16, 17).

When problems threaten your security in God, envision yourself in heaven, surrounded by such glory you can't contain your joy. The light of Jesus' presence makes you feel warmed and loved. You look back at the trials and sufferings you experienced on earth and suddenly you laugh. "Those problems seemed so intimidating at the time, but now I see how trivial they are in comparison with the joys of heaven."

I'm not minimizing the emotional or physical pain you may be experiencing. Maybe you've been evicted from your apartment and have no place to live. Maybe your car broke down, and you don't have money to repair it. Perhaps you're out of a job, and no one wants to hire you.

These are serious problems, but no matter how important they seem, heaven's glories will be so much greater. Even as you take the action God directs, stop a moment to consider that some day pure fellowship with Jesus Christ will be more important than anything else.

Problems are for our benefit and God's glory.

Dr. Hubert Davidson visited the noted poetess, Myra Brooks Welch, who perhaps is best known for her masterpiece, "The Touch of the Master's Hand." As he turned to leave her home, Myra Welch patted the arm of her wheelchair and said, "And I thank God for this." Imagine being grateful for a wheelchair! But her talent lay undiscovered prior to her wheelchair days. Rather than becoming bitter, she chose a better way, and a wonderful ministry opened new doors of blessings for her. Her poems have blessed the whole world.[3]

Romans 8:28 is still true. "And we know that in all things God works for the good of those who love him, who have been called according to his purpose."

I gain great comfort and security when I remember that everything entering my life is filtered through God's love. He knows exactly how I need to be challenged and stretched so that I'll grow closer to the image of Jesus Christ. David wrote, "It was good for me to be afflicted so that I might learn your decrees" (Ps. 119:71).

When life's unhappy circumstances throw you into a panic, believe that God will bring something good out of them. Such a realization will help you respond to problems like a secure woman.

WAITING ON THE LORD

Once we understand that problems fit into God's purpose for our lives, their power is defused, alleviating our fear. We then can respond in a godly manner. As previously stated, the first step of a godly response is to pray. We can then wait on the Lord for further direction.

When we rush ahead without waiting for guidance, we're like the insecure woman Dr. Peck refers to:

Once she became aware of a personal problem, she felt so discomfited that she demanded an immediate solution, and she was not willing to tolerate her discomfort long enough to analyze the problem. The solution to the problem represented gratification to her, but she was unable to delay this gratification for more than a minute or two, with the result that her solutions were usually inappropriate and her family in chronic turmoil.[4]

I remember a time when I reacted insecurely much like that woman. I planned to attend a child abuse conference in Sacramento, California, assuming that the organization with which I was associated would pay my way. When I received a speaking invitation from a Sacramento church during the same week as the conference, I quickly accepted, without consulting the Lord, even though church leaders said they were unable to pay my transportation expenses.

When I learned later my organization wouldn't pay my way either, I was miserable. With penitent tears, I asked the Lord's forgiveness for not seeking his direction. Larry and I decided we would pay my airfare to Sacramento to fulfill the speaking obligation, but I wouldn't attend the conference.

A few days later, the treasurer of the organization called me saying they would pay my way, after all. How grateful I was that the Lord had rescued me from my impatience.

When we're insecure, we're impatient. We grow nervous if we have to wait long for God to show us his plan. Insecurity causes us to demand fast solutions.

As we grow in security, we'll increasingly reject anxious thoughts such as: *God isn't going to take care of this. I'd better.* Waiting on God means holding steady until we have his direction, no matter how long it takes.

That doesn't mean we can't do anything without the Lord's specific leading. Life is filled with choices that require only common sense responses. Yesterday when I learned my neighbor was sick, I didn't pray for an hour before I took over a meal. Sometimes waiting on the Lord takes only a short, arrow prayer, but other times it involves a lengthy time of seeking him.

When Lorna sought the Lord's solution to a problem, she didn't know it would take a year of daily listening to him. She says of that time, "I couldn't seem to tap into God's strength. Don and I fought constantly. I stayed involved in Christian ministry but felt like a hypocrite.

"Because I had to find some answers, I eventually backed out of all ministry responsibilities. Each day at 7:00 a.m. when Don left for work, I turned on the answering machine and grabbed my Bible. I prayed, studied, cried, and looked to God. I attended church, and we occasionally socialized at night, but each weekday, I waited on God.

"I didn't start out with a time frame in mind, but as the days and then months passed, I couldn't wait for each morning and my time alone with the Lord.

"Something began to happen in my disagreements with Don. The day after a fight, God would give me specific insights about it. The next time we argued, instead of my usual selfish way of reacting, I could respond the way God wanted me to. Little by little, God healed many inner wounds from my past. Gradually joy replaced my pain, and a year after I started, I knew the Lord wanted me to become involved again in ministry."

Few of us can spend every day in prayer as Lorna did. Other responsibilities can't be put aside. But we *can* ask God for guidance in our problems as part of our daily quiet time—even if it means being locked in the bathroom for a few minutes while the kids pound on the door. Or we can find a babysitter for the morning and spend a half day of study and meditation at the park.

We can choose to wait for God's solution to problems with a peaceful, trusting heart, knowing he will respond in his timing. That's security.

F.B. Meyer writes,

Never act in a panic, nor allow man to dictate to thee. Calm thyself and be still. Force thyself into the quiet of thy closet until the pulse beats normally and the scare has ceased to disturb.

When thou art most eager to act is the time when thou wilt make the most pitiable mistakes.

Do not say in thine heart what thou wilt or wilt not do, but wait upon thy God until He makes known His way.

So long as that way is hidden, it is clear that there is no need of action, and that He accounts Himself responsible for all the results of keeping thee where thou art.[5]

WHEN GOD ACTS TOO SLOWLY

If it seems God acts too slowly, remember he sees everything from an eternal perspective.

God never hurries. He takes his time in developing us for our earthly calling as well as for eternity. Moses was 80 when he began his major task, and his preparation included 40 years of oblivion in the wilderness. After David was chosen and anointed to be king, God groomed him for 13 years as he wandered about hiding in caves to escape capture and death. After God removed his opponent, one of the twelve tribes of Israel crowned him king; it took seven more years before the whole nation accepted him. Consider also the apostle Paul. We read little about him until fourteen years after his conversion, when at about the age of 48 he was launched into his life's work. Even in our age of rapid change and instant everything, God continues to prefer quality rather than speed in developing his people.[6]

Dr. A.H. Strong says something similar, "When God wants to make an oak, he takes a hundred years, but when he wants to make a squash, he takes six months."[7]

Do we want to be God's oak or his squash? Our patience while God works will develop the character and strength of an oak tree.

While you're seeking the Lord for his guidance, you'll grow even closer to him, for you'll be spending more time in his presence.

PUZZLE PIECES OF SOLUTIONS

As you spend time with God, he will provide a solution. However, it may not be the answer you hoped for. Usually, the solution comes in glimpses and pieces.

Connie's husband left her for another woman. "I can't believe this is happening," she told me recently. "I'm just trusting God will bring good out of it as he promises. If we get back together, maybe Phil will become the spiritual head of our home."

Connie's husband vacillates between Connie and his girlfriend. Even though Connie prays for a quick solution, each day she must choose her reactions toward her husband and cope with her children's insecurities. Each small guidance is another piece of a puzzle, but each piece isn't given in order. She has one piece for the center, another for the right-hand corner, and another for the left border. At the present time, the puzzle is still incomplete.

How can we stay secure—feeling loved and reacting confidently—when we're only given a few puzzle pieces at a time? According to Evelyn Christenson:

This view of God as an omniscient Father comes into focus very clearly as the years pass. One of the advantages of growing older is that we can look back and see that God has not made a single mistake in our lives. Maybe we'll have to get to heaven before we understand some things, but it's exciting to recognize as the years come and go that everything has worked together for good if we have really loved Him.[8]

The way God works out a solution is similar to the way a plant grows. A little seed—a thought—begins to take root. Then the seed sprouts with some specific ideas. Sometimes a leaf appears, but it doesn't look right, so we pinch it off. Other times, nothing grows and we feel frustrated. We can't see it yet, but God is working in someone's life to bring him to our aid or he may be strengthening a character quality in us. He's causing the roots to grow below the surface.

"In his heart a man plans his course, but the Lord determines his steps" (Prov. 16:9). The growth process continues and we pray, consider the alternatives, reject some, and encourage others to grow. Eventually, the plant is large and ready to bear fruit; God opens the door and, together, we put the plan into action.

The growth of a solution occurred in Tammy's family. Tammy's son, Kevin, experienced more and more problems as he progressed through elementary school. In the early grades, Tammy and her husband Kyle attributed his low grades to shyness. Kevin was tested for a hearing disorder, but the tests were inconclusive. Later they learned that Kevin had been given the wrong test.

"Why can't this be solved more quickly?" Tammy lamented to Kyle. "We pray and ask God to guide us, but we have no clear-cut answers."

Kyle replied, "Honey, I don't know what to do, but since Kevin's working at grade level, let's let things go for awhile." Tammy agreed.

Several years passed, and Kevin was still struggling in the fifth grade. Tammy and Kyle became convinced Kevin needed help. They contacted the school and requested that the school psychologist test Kevin for learning disabilities. The psychologist put Kevin on the waiting list but didn't have time to test him before school ended. So Tammy and Kyle waited.

Finally, when Kevin entered sixth grade, he was tested and found to have Attention Deficit Disorder Syndrome for which there is no cure. Tammy and Kyle have now arranged for a math tutor and counseling for Kevin.

Tammy says, "So many times we've pleaded for a concrete resolution to this whole thing. I've shed lots of tears, but somewhere, somehow we believe God will use this for good. God continues to remind us that the goal isn't to get rid of all problems, but instead to trust him as we work through them."

God has answered many of Tammy and Kyle's prayers. Yet, their problem is long-term, and the Lord is using it to strengthen their faith in him. They've remained confident in his power to guide them.

TAKING ACTION

You're facing a problem. You've prayed about it and waited for God's direction. You sense his leading in some ways, and now it's time for you to step out in faith and proceed with the plan he's revealed.

If you need a job, for example, you may update your resumé and send it out. You may check the newspaper want ads and friends for possible leads. If the Lord is directing you toward a career change, you may need to buy different clothing.

Your attitude during this planning and preparing distinguishes you as a secure or insecure woman. The insecure woman prepares with an attitude of turmoil, doubting that God can lead her. But the secure woman experiences an inner confidence in the midst of her activity, believing God will provide. Isaiah 26:3 encourages her: "You will keep in perfect peace him whose mind is steadfast because he trusts in you."

My friend Jennifer Botkin-Maher, author of *Nice Girls Don't Get Raped*, experienced that perfect peace as she looked for a job. Should she minister through classes and seminars or use her nursing degree in the medical profession? Should she write full-time? She sent out resumés, but for two months, nothing happened. All the while, she prayed and exercised patience, but she still took action, even to the point of buying new nursing clothing.

Now, several months later, she has seen God's answer: all three, actually. She has a nursing job on call, she continues to write articles and books, and she teaches adult education classes through several colleges. Because those jobs aren't consistent money-makers, Jennifer continues to keep her "mind steadfast" in the Lord.

Jennifer took action as she sensed God's leading.

God doesn't want us to be shaken "like a wave of the sea, blown and tossed by the wind" (Jas. 1:6). Instead, he is pleased when we say with the psalmist, "When I felt secure, I said, 'I will never be shaken' " (Ps. 30:6).

The next time a problem faces us, let's remember to wait on God for the answer and to take action when he leads. Then we'll stand strong as secure women.

4

...

A Secure Woman Is Encouraged During Cycles of Change

On New Year's Eve when I was in the eighth grade, I took a bath to symbolically cleanse myself from all my sins the previous year. I wanted so much to be pure in God's eyes, and I believed this would show him how serious I was about being good.

Even though I'd never committed a really "bad" sin, such as murder, I was nevertheless aware of my unloving reactions and thoughts. Why couldn't I behave better—even perfectly? I was sure that was the only way God could totally love and accept me.

At midnight, I lay soaking in a hot, bubbly tub, listening to horns tooting, people yelling, and the party next door spilling out into the street.

"God, please forgive me for everything I did wrong last

year, and help me not do anything wrong in 1962," I prayed. When I stepped out of the tub, I felt clean and pure, and I determined I would stay that way for the next year. Climbing into bed dressed in a freshly washed nightgown and covered by clean sheets, I fell asleep feeling secure.

When I awakened the next morning, I told myself confidently, "I'm finally going to get my life together." The morning went well until I discovered my younger sister Karen using my new colored pencils.

I felt an instant rage. "Get out of my things," I screamed at her. When I calmed down, the realization hit me like a truck. *Oh, no! I blew it again.* All my hopes for perfection drained away, replaced by discouragement. I was *never* going to be a good girl.

All my life, I've wanted to be good—to be perfect. In junior high and high school, perfection to me was personified in my best friend's mother, Marie. She was perfect, I reasoned, because if the clothes she sewed for my friend weren't exactly right, she ripped out the seams and started over. I, on the other hand, would wear anything I made as long as it stayed in one piece. Therefore, I couldn't be perfect.

My unconscious desire for perfection revealed itself in many ways. For instance, I often sat quietly while adults carried on conversations around me, hoping someone would say, "Oh, look at Kathy. Isn't she a good little girl?" Because of my low self-esteem, I desperately strived for approval. My security did not come from within; rather, it depended on other people's view of me.

If only I could achieve perfection, I wouldn't have to struggle anymore. I could just sit back and enjoy life. I spent most of my childhood and teenage years striving for perfection.

Because I didn't understand that life is a cycle of constant change, I also thought God wanted me to be perfect. And since I continued to sin, I reasoned, he couldn't accept me *yet*. But one day, I would somehow become good *enough* so he could accept me. Though few of these thoughts were conscious, they definitely influenced my attitudes toward life.

When I became a Christian at age eighteen, I knew that God had forgiven my sins, and his power was available to me. Then why did I continue to be critical of others? Why did I store up bitterness? *Why aren't I perfect now?* I wondered again and again. Verses such as "Be perfect and complete, lacking in nothing" (Jas. 1:4 NASB) haunted me. How was I ever going to be perfect and complete when even with God's power I continued to sin?

Later, when I heard a paraphrase of James 1:4, "Have a balanced personality and spiritual maturity," I began to hope. This sounded attainable. At last I had a measuring rod for God's working in my life. Now I realized a balanced personality and spiritual maturity weren't attained instantly, but by a process of growth. Relief flooded me. After years of failing to achieve security by striving for perfection, I no longer had unrealistic expectations hanging over my head. Knowing that life is a continuing cycle of stretching, changing, and growing, I could accept myself as imperfect.

THE PROCESS OF GROWTH

God used this same process of growth in his relationship with the Israelites. In Exodus 23, he promised them success in conquering the Canaanites, Hivites, and Hittites as they possessed the promised land of Canaan. Exodus 23:29, 30 says, "I will not drive them out in a single year, because the land would become desolate and the wild animals too numerous for you. Little by little I will drive them out before you, until you have increased enough to take possession of the land."

He says the same thing to us: "I will not give you an instantaneous deliverance from every sin, because this would make you proud, and you would think you don't need me anymore. Instead, I'll show you an area that needs correction, and when you've grown in that area, I'll show you another. That way you'll always stay dependent on me, and you will learn principles that you can share with others."

Recently, as I finally gained some self-control in my overeating of sugar, this was impressed upon me again. I praised the Lord for the success he'd given me. But not long after, a glaring awareness of my unloving attitude toward a friend stared me in the face. The ways we must change will never end, I realized anew.

This can be discouraging, especially for the perfectionist. The perfectionist—the insecure woman—wants changes right now, without any struggle or action on her part. She can also become discouraged when she realizes that she's never going to "arrive." There will always be something she needs to work on or improve or change. This cycle will continue for the rest of her life, but the insecure woman doesn't like to face that fact. She looks at this cycle of change as negative instead of positive. Becoming depressed, she shouts, "God, why do I have to go through these painful problems? Why do I have to constantly change? Why can't you just make me perfect and be done with it?"

IDENTIFYING THE PERFECTIONIST

Dr. David D. Burns, clinical assistant professor of psychiatry at the University of Pennsylvania Medical School comments, "Perfectionists are people who strain compulsively toward impossible goals and measure their self-worth entirely in terms of their achievements. As a result, they are terrified by the prospect of failure. They feel driven and, at the same time, unrewarded by their accomplishments."[1]

Dr. Burns identifies several attitudes the perfectionist has: all or nothing thinking ("If I can't do it perfectly, I won't do it at all"), believing a negative event will be repeated endlessly ("I'll never get this right"), fear of rejection, persistent feelings of loneliness, and disturbances in personal relationships with others.

"Much of the perfectionist's difficulties, the experts say, stem from insecurity," says Wayne Coffey. "Perfectionists don't like themselves as they are, and they're sure other people won't, either. Consequently, to gain acceptance, they feel they have to perform in a perfect or nearly perfect way, thus linking their self image to their ability to do well at a given task."[2]

If you suspect you are a perfectionist, take the following test by checking the statements that apply to you:

• If I can't do something exactly right, I won't do it at all.
• I often start things I don't finish.
• It's hard for me to relax even after my work is done.
• I am often amazed at the incompetence of others.
• I can't stand it when things are out of place.
• I find unpredictability vexing, if not intolerable.
• I have a burning need to set things right.
• I worry a lot about why I haven't done better.
• Any kind of personal failure is the worst thing I can think of.
• It seems to me that standards are slipping everywhere.

If you checked more than three of the above, you tend to be a perfectionist.[3]

OUR POSITION IN CHRIST

The secure woman fights perfectionism by recognizing the difference between her position in Christ and her practice on earth. Her position in Christ, a result of making Jesus her Savior and Lord, is one of being completely accepted and forgiven by God. Because she wears the robe of Jesus' righteousness, God sees her as perfect! Hebrews 10:14 says, "Because by one sacrifice he has made perfect forever those who are being made holy."

If you have received Jesus Christ as your Savior, then you also are totally accepted by God. You have the assurance that God sees you as perfect because he looks at you through Jesus' redemptive death on the cross. He requires nothing more of you in order for you to qualify "to share in the inheritance of the saints in the kingdom of light" (Col. 1:12).

Because of your position in Christ, your inheritance includes many wonderful benefits. Here are just a few:

Completion (Col. 2:10)

Spiritual blessings (Eph. 1:3)

Wisdom, righteousness, holiness, and redemption (1 Cor. 1:30)

Justification (Rom. 5:1)

No condemnation (Rom. 8:1)

Blamelessness (1 Cor. 1:8)

Promise of God's working (Phil. 1:6)

Forgiveness (1 John 1:9)

OUR PERFORMANCE ON EARTH

What an exciting list of advantages for every child of God. But the next logical question is: If I'm perfect in

God's sight and have access to all these wonderful things, why am I still not perfect here on earth?

Our Christian walk is a struggle between our old sin nature and our new spiritual nature. Both want to rule. Even though our "position in Christ" is perfect, our performance on earth is not. Our performance is still influenced by old habits and behaviors that still grip us. Old attitudes continue to influence us. Even the apostle Paul said, "Not that I have already obtained all this, or have already been made perfect, but I press on to take hold of that for which Christ Jesus took hold of me" (Phil. 3:12).

The secure woman understands her position in Christ as perfect and her walk on earth as a cycle of change that will continue throughout her lifetime. She views the cycle of change positively as she sees her struggles resulting in good things. First, because the answers are not within herself, she continues to seek God. Second, she never becomes smug or proud; she knows she can't ever say she has arrived. Third, she's less tempted to judge others for their imperfections . . . after all, she isn't perfect either.

Finally, and most importantly, the cycle of change forces the secure woman to view life from God's perspective: as a step to the higher goal of heaven. Most people have an earthly perspective—they view life as the end in itself. But God views life from an eternal perspective. God wants us to see that life is only preparation for spending eternity with him. The difficult circumstances and people who stretch and challenge us are meant to help us change and grow.

THE SECURE WOMAN'S GOAL

I often think of people as rough, uncut diamonds and God as the diamond cutter intent on producing beautiful gems. Diamonds are formed when carbon is crystallized under tremendous heat and pressure. They are the hardest substance known on earth. The name diamond is derived from the Greek word *adamas* meaning "invincible." Uncut diamonds have a greasy luster and are dull; their many beautiful qualities are unseen. However, the diamond cutter cuts them in such a way that their fire and brilliance will be evident to all. To accomplish this, the cutter must eliminate imperfections, such as cracks, flaws, and cloudiness by "cutting" or "sawing."

Before he begins his work, he carefully examines the stone, marking how it should be cut. Next, he cements the stone into a holder. In the old-fashioned method, the cutter strikes the stone with a cleaving iron, an instrument resembling a heavy, blunt knife. This requires great skill because too hard a blow applied in a wrong direction could ruin the stone. In modern practice, diamonds are usually "sawed" by thin metal disks.

After the diamond has been cut or sawed, different "facets" are polished into it to bring out its inherent beauty. Polishing involves holding the diamond against a wheel that is charged with a mixture of diamond dust and oil. The diamond is moved many times as each facet is polished into its surface. When the diamond cutter finishes, the diamond is judged on its color, shape, weight, and absence of flaws. A valuable diamond is transparent, has high luster with spectral colors, and resists scratching and the attack of acids and alkalis.

The process a diamond goes through is an analogy of the cycle of change a woman goes through to achieve and maintain security. Like an uncut diamond, she has hidden qualities. She isn't transparent; often she's "cloudy." She only sees within herself and is blind to the needs of others. Too insecure to risk rejection, she can't allow God's "warmth" to be conducted through her to help and love others. Unable to resist stress, she is easily discouraged and defensive. Life often "scratches," irritates, and angers her.

But God, as a woman's "diamond cutter," sees the potential inner beauty and security in her. As a way of making her turn to him, he allows her to experience tremendous heat and pressure. When she submits to his skilled "cutting," he slices away her rough edges, "sawing" and "cleaving" her by allowing certain circumstances in her life. People criticize her. People disappoint her. Her plans don't materialize. Her hopes are crushed.

As she sees the results of her wrong reactions, these circumstances become opportunities for her to learn new responses. As God's skillful hands move her around, the "facets" of his character are strengthened and revealed within her: love, joy, peace, patience, kindness, goodness, faithfulness, gentleness, and self-control (Gal. 5:22, 23).

The secure woman participates in this process of cutting and polishing through a four-step cycle of change: counting the cost of changing, keeping an eternal perspective, recommitting to the task of changing, and correcting areas that contribute to insecurity.

COUNTING THE COST

When a woman counts the cost of changing, she either decides the goal is too hard to reach, or she decides, "Yes, it's worth it. I want to change and grow even though it's a painful process."

My friend, Carol, has made such a decision as she painfully seeks God's healing following her discovery of her husband Ken's cocaine addiction. When she sought Christian therapy, her counselor confronted her with her dysfunctional responses to life. For the first time, Carol is beginning to understand that she unknowingly lived the life of a victim.

"I was completely caught off guard when the counselor told me I was helping my husband be an addict by my blindness to the problem," she told me. "At first, I flatly refused to face the problem because I love my husband and want us to be a strong Christian family. Besides, I couldn't understand how my reactions helped his addiction. How dare the counselor blame me for Ken's problem. He's responsible for his own choices.

"But after several therapy sessions, I began to see how the whole family was in this together. When this truth hit me, I cried and cried. I didn't want to be responsible for my part of the problem. I wanted to blame it all on Ken.

"Now I know I've contributed to my family's dysfunctionalism. It's certainly not all my fault, but I've helped. It's very painful to examine my reactions and learn how to operate without a victim's mind-set. I am determined, though, to stick it out, no matter what it takes. The Lord has helped me so far and I know he'll continue."

Like Carol, the secure woman isn't afraid to count the cost—to think about the price she will have to pay to change—because she's assured God is with her.

Counting the cost of changing may involve carefully considering the advantages and disadvantages of such a change. Although God is primarily interested in giving us life and bringing character changes, he also is concerned about job changes, plans to marry or divorce, moving to a new location, buying a new car, etc. He can guide us as we think through the consequences of our potential decisions. He wants us to count the cost and look to him for his plan for us.

KEEPING AN ETERNAL PERSPECTIVE

As we consider what God's plans may be, we must always keep in mind the difference between earthly and eternal perspectives.

EARTHLY PERSPECTIVE	ETERNAL PERSPECTIVE
People should meet my needs.	God will meet my true needs, not necessarily my wants (Phil 4:19).
My purpose in life is to enjoy myself.	My purpose is to please and glorify God (Eph. 1:6).
I want to avoid trials and problems .	I can welcome trials and problems as friends and grow through them (Jas. 1:2).
I'm going to get all I can for me.	I can serve others because I receive so much from God (Eph. 2:10).
I want to do my own thing.	I want to obey and seek God's will (Matt. 6:33).
Controlling the people and things around me will make me secure.	I can trust God to work in the lives of others (Rom. 12:19).

Keeping an eternal perspective, rather than an earthly one, helps us grow in security.

COMMITTING AND RECOMMITTING

Once we've counted the cost with the eternal perspective in mind, and begin to head in a certain direction, the secure woman must commit and recommit herself to the task of changing. At times, she will lash out in anger instead of being patient. At times, she will feel good rehashing hurts instead of being forgiving. And at times, she will try to force people to do things her way instead of communicating her needs, then trusting God to fulfill them. It is when she realizes she has fallen short of her goals that discouragement can take away her determination to change. Then she needs to recommit herself to the process of growing.

Recommitting involves asking for forgiveness for the wrong choices she makes. The secure woman claims 1 John 1:9: "If we confess our sins, he is faithful and just and will forgive us our sins and purify us from all unrighteousness." Even though she may need to repeatedly ask forgiveness for wrong choices, she is confident that she's in God's will and the cycle of change. At times, she may think, "Oh, I can't ask God to forgive me again for the same thing." She's forgotten that when he forgives us, he no longer counts it against us and, in effect, has forgotten our past sins.

When you feel discouraged because change doesn't happen quickly or easily, choose to respond like a secure woman. Recommit yourself to continue the process of growth God wants in your life.

CORRECTING AREAS OF INSECURITY

Finally, the secure woman corrects the areas that contribute to insecurity in her life. She is sensitive to God's leading for correction, is willing to change, and trusts that God will continue the good work in her (Phil. 1:6).

Some areas in which God wants each woman to change so she can grow in security are to:

Trust in him instead of herself (Prov. 3:5, 6).

Pray instead of worrying (Phil. 4:6).

Be humble instead of proud (1 Pet. 5:6).

Operate in God's power instead of her own (Phil. 4:13).

Be assured of salvation instead of doubting (1 John 5:13).

Put God's will before her own (Matt. 6:33).

Depend on God to fulfill her needs instead of looking to other people (Phil 4:19).

If you have perfectionistic tendencies, Sandra Simpson LeSourd, author of *The Compulsive Woman*, has some suggestions for overcoming them:

1. Begin by accepting your mistake-prone nature. No one is perfect.

2. Make a list of the advantages and disadvantages of requiring flawlessness in yourself. You'll be surprised at how few advantages there are to rigid thinking.

3. See the difference between perfectionism and the healthy pursuit of excellence.

4. Reduce some of your goals. Dare to be average for a time.

5. Be willing to experience anxiety about loose ends. These feelings will pass if you let some things slide.

6. If you're an extreme perfectionist, consider therapy.[4]

The many areas of our thinking that need to change may seem overwhelming. That's why we need God's strengthening help. Recently, I received several calls from friends, requesting prayer for different, overwhelming circumstances. Barbara thought she was having a miscarriage. Could she trust God to do the right thing for this baby? Janel recently had a baby and her two-year-old daughter cries most of the day because of jealousy and frustration. Could she believe that God would give her the strength to discipline patiently? Sally and her husband had begun to remodel their house when he lost his job. Could

God provide for their financial needs?

Each situation represented a woman going through the cycle of change. In each, the diamond of her life was being cut and shaped to the four criteria that measure the value of a diamond: brilliant color that reflects God's presence; a shape that reveals character qualities; weight that has the strength to reject unloving reactions; and the absence of flaws that represents God's power.

Do you see yourself as a diamond that God is changing into a beautiful representation of himself? You can be a secure woman and not grow discouraged when the problems and pressures of life try to make you insecure. Knowing God is using them for beauty in your life is the basis of real security. Though the process will never be finished in this life, you can be a complete and secure woman. Life's cycle of change will result in goodness and beauty . . . as found in a diamond.

5
...

A Secure Woman
Is Protected
Against Opposition

One warm California day our family decided to go to the fair. While we enjoyed the amusement rides and exhibits, one display in particular impressed me: a heated, egg-shaped container held thirty eggs in various stages of hatching. Fascinated children and adults crowded around its windows watching and hoping to see one chick free itself from the confines of its shell.

How much energy it took for that chick to peck steadily away at the shell until a tiny hole appeared! Then, little by little, the struggling chick continued to peck ... peck ... peck its way to freedom. Seeing the chick's heavy breathing, I wondered, *How in the world is he ever going to have enough strength to be completely hatched? He'll die before he gets out of that shell.* Yet the chick continued to laboriously peck with an inner strength and perseverance I admired.

Then something curious happened. One of the already-hatched chicks began pecking at it. He grabbed a tuft of feathers and yanked. *No, No, that's not helping!* I thought. *Leave him alone, or you'll kill him.*

Talk about having more than you can handle! The exhausted chick not only had to cope with a very hard shell, but with the other chick's pecking at him. It would be a miracle if he survived. I left the display wondering how many of the chicks would make it into the world.

Later, I thought of how those chicks were a picture of a woman striving for security. She, too, labors to break the shell of insecurity that prevents her from leading a fulfilled life. As she grapples with the process of growth, little by little she frees herself from restraints in her life that prevent her from accepting God's security.

Like that struggling chick who was pecked by another chick, the woman seeking security may be "pecked" by other people. Even if she doesn't realize it, she can become discouraged by the disapproving comments of others who don't understand her desire to be secure. Perhaps they comment, "You believe that hocus-pocus religious stuff? You aren't going to become a fanatic, are you?" "Religion is just a crutch." "Obviously, you're too far gone to rebuild your life." "Security is an impossibility for anyone."

Sometimes, comments come from Christians who lack understanding. Perhaps seeing someone else gaining security makes their own inadequacies more glaring. Deep down inside, they know they should be striving for the same thing but don't know how.

A stronger oppositional force is that of Satan's spirit world. He doesn't want us to succeed because our success will glorify God.

Finally, there's the opposition from within ourselves. We can oppose ourselves without even realizing it. We may have had experiences in our past of which we are not aware, but they may psychologically influence us. Unconsciously, we may be threatened by the possibility of gaining security. We've gone beyond our "comfort zone" where we are accustomed to being, even though it's a "zone" of insecurity.

Regardless of the oppositions—people, spiritual forces, or ourselves—there is protection from their attacks.

OPPOSITION FROM OTHERS

Let's first look at opposition from people. Their opposition may be overt, such as someone saying, "You don't believe depending on Jesus will help you, do you?" Or it may be more subtle: a raised eyebrow when we talk about our new-found faith; a sigh of impatience when we mention the Bible; bored silence when we mention God.

Opposition may take the form of anger if we assert ourselves when formerly we were unassertive. It could also be gossip, "Hey, have you talked to Suzie lately? She's really gone crazy with this religious trip."

This kind of opposition cuts us to the quick. In our enthusiasm, we thought that everyone would be thrilled about our new thinking. It's hard for us to believe that anyone would disagree with our desire to become a secure and happy person.

But opposition isn't new or original. From one of the earliest stories in Scripture, we hear Job say to the friends who have come to "help" him: "How long will you torment me and crush me with words?" (Job 19:2).

Lisa experienced that kind of pressure. She had grown in her faith in God, but the pressures at home were enormous. Her husband didn't want her to attend church, and work made it impossible for her to attend other church functions during the day. She did attend a class I taught, but when the class ended, her husband refused to let her participate in other church activities. Lisa was like the chick trying to free itself and finding people "pecking" at *her* rather than at her shell of insecurity. Instead of support, she received discouragement.

Perhaps you feel like Lisa. People around you make fun of you when you talk about your growing faith in God. Your husband doesn't want you to attend church. Your children complain when you encourage them to join youth activities. Instead of love and support, you are showered with criticism and condemnation.

As I said before, our growth may create feelings of insecurity in others. Our security may threaten their control over us. If insecurity has kept us from being assertive in the past, then our new security and assertiveness will free us from their power over us. We will no longer be their "yes people." Now we communicate our needs and opinions. They don't appreciate our taking charge of our life. Our strength may also reveal their insecurities. A secure woman may momentarily feel unsure of herself when she is assaulted by such pressure, but she can remain encouraged and continue to grow.

CODEPENDENCY

Another area that can hinder us is our codependency. While we may think we're reacting correctly to the insecure people around us, codependency can stunt our ability to grow secure in the Lord.

In her book, *Codependent No More*, Melody Beattie, writes, "A codependent person is one who has let another person's behavior affect him or her, and who is obsessed with controlling that person's behavior."[1]

Codependency takes many forms. Julie is married to an abusive, alcoholic husband, but she keeps thinking, "If I were just a better wife, he wouldn't have this problem. I'll fix his favorite meal for dinner, and maybe he won't leave for the bar."

Marcia's son is addicted to cocaine. She feels paralyzed by his problem and wonders, "What did I do wrong as a mother? Why didn't I see the addiction coming? I'll search his room every day and make sure he doesn't use that stuff."

Freddie is a compassionate Christian who believes her mission from God is to help those who are needy. Her latest project is Silvia, who just called, desperate because she needs a ride to her doctor's office. Freddie promises to help her, ignoring the messiness of her own home, and drives off, thinking, *I said I'd work on that project for Jim, but if I don't help Silvia, who will?*

Melody Beattie describes this unique group:

Most codependents were obsessed with other people. With great precision and detail, they could recite long lists of the addict's deeds and misdeeds: what he or she thought, felt, did, and said; and what he or she didn't think, feel, do, and say. The codependents knew what the alcoholic or addict should and shouldn't do. And they wondered extensively why he or she didn't do it.

Yet these codependents who had such great insight into others couldn't see themselves. They didn't know what they were feeling. They weren't sure what they thought. And they didn't know what, if anything, they could do to solve their problems—if, indeed, they had any problems other than the alcoholics.[2]

If you're codependent and being robbed of security because of it, it may be difficult for you to identify yourself in that description. "After all," you may think, "I'm not that bad. Of course I keep tabs on my husband's drinking. If I don't, he'll go on a binge. And as far as the help I give Stephanie, that's only what any Christian would do, isn't it?"

Maybe. Maybe not. Take the following test, and see if it gives you any insights into your own behavior.

TEST YOURSELF

___My good feelings about who I am stem from being liked by you.

___My good feelings about who I am stem from receiving approval from you.

___Your struggles affect my serenity. My mental attention focuses on solving or relieving your pain.

___My mental attention is focused on pleasing you.

___My mental attention is focused on protecting you.

___My mental attention is focused on manipulating you to "do it my way."

___My self-esteem is bolstered by solving your problems.

___My self-esteem is bolstered by relieving your pain.

___My own hobbies and interests are put aside. My time is spent sharing your interests and hobbies.

___Your clothing and personal appearance is dictated by my desires because I feel you are a reflection of me.

___Your behavior is dictated by my desires because I feel you are a reflection of me.

___I am not aware of how I feel. I am aware of how you feel. I am not aware of what I want. I ask you what you want. If I am not aware of something, I assume.

___The dreams I have for my future are linked to you.

___My fear of rejection determines what I say or do.

___My fear of your anger determines what I say or do.

___I use giving as a way of feeling safe in our relationship.

___My social circle diminishes as I involve myself with you.

___I put my values aside in order to connect with you.

___I value your opinion and way of doing things more than my own.

___The quality of my life is in relation to the quality of yours.[3]

Any woman will see herself in some of these statements, but if you identified yourself in many or most of these attitudes, there's a strong possibility you are codependent.

If so, you will have a hard time developing your own security because even though you don't know it, others around you are opposing you. They don't want you to become secure enough in yourself to break their control over you. Instead of realizing that they are responsible for their own actions and decisions, they want to continue to make you feel responsible for their happiness . . . or sanity . . . or staying drug-free . . . or being alcohol-free.

Breaking yourself of these dependency patterns may not be simple, but it can be done with God's help. In order to do so, you must be committed in your pursuit of security despite the opposition of others. God wants you to grow, and he will provide the support you need as you seek him. In the following pages, you'll discover practical ideas for dealing with other people's opposition.

OPPOSITION FROM SPIRITUAL FORCES

In your travels toward security, don't be surprised when spiritual forces try to hinder your growing faith. The Bible warns us of a destructive spiritual agent: Satan. "Be self-controlled and alert. Your enemy, the devil, prowls around like a roaring lion looking for someone to devour. Resist him, standing firm in the faith" (1 Pet. 5:8, 9).

Satan is not a cartoon character with horns and a pointed tail. In fact, he is a beautiful archangel who, because he opposed God, was cast out of heaven. Since then, he has attemped to achieve his prime purpose: to frustrate people's growth in God. The apostle Paul writes to the believers at Corinth, "But I am afraid that just as Eve was deceived by the serpent's cunning, your minds may somehow be led astray from your sincere and pure devotion to Christ" (2 Cor. 11:3).

Satan wants to prevent us from experiencing the security of personal faith in the Lord. He wants to hinder our simple trust in God for everything. He doesn't want us to have relief from worry, strength to cope with stress, or any other life-changing joys. Instead, the enemy lies: "Depending on God is foolishness. No modern woman would put her life in his hands. He'll only make you a wishy-washy nobody who lets everyone walk all over you. Live life to the hilt; do things your way. You can't enjoy life as a Christian, only sissies need a crutch like religion." Satan's tools of opposition are discouragement, depression, deceit, dissatisfaction, and disagreement.

Although Satan is a powerful enemy, Christians have a more powerful God who strengthens and protects us from the enemy's devious tactics. Romans 8:38, 39 assures us, "For I am convinced that neither death nor life, neither angels nor demons, neither the present nor the future, nor any powers, neither height nor depth, not anything else in all creation, will be able to separate us from the love of God that is in Christ Jesus our Lord." As secure women, we need not fear when destructive spiritual forces try to discourage and undermine us. We are protected and secure in God's love.

Spiritual forces are at work around us. When my friend, Judy, was hospitalized because of complications from multiple sclerosis and given a new medication, she experienced hallucinations. One day while I was visiting her, she suddenly asked, "Did you hear what the nurses said?" I looked around and didn't see anyone in the room, and the nurses' station was too far down the hall for any talking to be heard.

I replied, "I can't hear anyone except us, Judy."

"Oh, I can," she whispered. "They're talking about me. One just said, 'I wish she'd die.' And another said, 'Let's get rid of her.' What am I going to do? They want to kill me."

I had never heard Judy talk this way, and it frightened me. I tried to assure her that what she was "hearing" was only her mind, but she wouldn't be persuaded. I began to pray for Judy's protection and for a calm heart. I asked God to rebuke Satan and keep him from influencing Judy's thinking. As I prayed, I felt the power of God's strength making my words real and effective.

After we prayed, I told Judy, "When those negative voices come into your mind, think about the things that are real here, like the TV, the floor, your bed, even your Bible. Tell yourself they're real, but the voices aren't."

Judy agreed, and after visiting a while longer, I left, continuing to pray for her on the way home. Shortly after I arrived, Judy called to say she had experienced a release from the depression and the hallucinations. For the next several days, she continued to focus on the real things in her room, and eventually she was able to totally block out the false voices.

In this instance, Satan used the medication Judy was taking to cause hallucinations and depression. Prayer made the difference; Judy was protected even though she continued to receive the medication.

Sometimes, though, we will need to do more than just pray. Fasting or staying with the person involved may be needed. If we are the ones being attacked, we may need to ask for another Christian's help. Additionally, we should break any contacts we have with people involved in the occult and purge our house from any items used in occult practices.

As shown in my experience with Judy, we have strength and power from God even to fight destructive spiritual forces. The Bible assures us, "The one who is in you [God] is greater than the one who is in the world [Satan]" (1 John 4:4).

OPPOSITION FROM OURSELVES

Our final opposition comes from within ourselves and is often the greatest cause of our insecurity. In many ways we can be our own worst enemies. Our "self-talk" or dwelling on past experiences can limit our growth toward security. Low self-esteem can discourage us from believing God loves us. These self-destructive forces can obstruct and slow our steps toward security, even when we aren't conscious of what we're doing to ourselves.

Although Alicia didn't know it, her past prevented her from becoming more secure. After reading my book *Healing the Angry Heart* she wrote to tell me her story.

When Alicia was in her early thirties, migraine headaches continually kept her in bed. After her doctors could find nothing physically wrong with her, they suggested she consult a psychiatrist. At first she laughed, then she became angry. "How dare they think all this is in my head! I haven't had any traumatic experiences in my life. Other than these horrible headaches, my life is great."

No sooner had she said the words than she realized that the truth wasn't quite that rosy. Thinking back over the past few years, she realized that she was easily depressed and insecure in her relationship with her husband. Issues that had previously never bothered her now became reasons for angry fights. Could something she didn't recognize be bothering her?

Afraid, she pushed the thoughts aside and decided to cope with the headaches as best she could. But when her medicine lost its effectiveness, she became desperate and finally made an appointment with a Christian psychologist.

Several months of counseling enabled Alicia to remember more about her childhood. Then suddenly one day the memory of her uncle's molesting her when she was six flooded her mind.

" 'No, no, it can't be true,' I kept saying," Alicia related to me. "All the horrible feelings of that experience returned in full force. I again felt the shame, guilt, and anger. *Why did he do it? What did I do to deserve such treatment? I shouldn't have gone with him that day to the store. It's all my fault.* I slumped to the floor and pounded my fists on my thighs. I hated myself.

"Then as my counselor prayed with me, I was able to see the experience from an adult's viewpoint. 'Wait a minute,' I told myself. 'I didn't do anything wrong. He's the one who molested *me*. He forced himself on *me*. It's not my fault!'

"I can't tell you the relief that flooded my spirit. It was as if God removed a one hundred pound weight off my inner being. My tears turned from hot, angry tears, to tears of freedom. I still couldn't forgive my uncle, but just knowing I wasn't responsible comforted me so much."

Alicia began the healing process that day, and it continued for several months as she learned to forgive her uncle who had died three years earlier. Now she rarely has headaches.

"That healing was just the beginning," Alicia writes. "Facing that experience taught me that I repress a lot of my feelings. I'm continuing in counseling to learn how to be honest about them and to respond appropriately when people hurt me."

Such extreme circumstances do not happen to all of us, but this example can give us insight into how experiences from our past prevent us from growing as a secure person.

Once we become aware of the opposition we face, what can we do to protect ourselves? The secret is a balance between action and trust. Let's look at how to do that.

TAKING ACTION

Taking action presents us with the possibilities of seeking Christian counseling, reading self-help books, being open to healing past hurts through an inner healing, and asking trusted friends to help and encourage us. All these options can help us grow emotionally.

I experienced my own inner healing recently while attending a mother-daughter retreat. At the closing session, the speaker, Marilyn Meberg, shared some steps of inner healing. At first, I rejected the idea, yet I found myself touched and tears coming to my eyes.

At the conclusion, a woman I'd met at the conference turned to me. "Did something she said touch you?" she asked. I admitted it had, but I didn't know why. Then she shared how she had gone through an inner healing that had dealt with her father's death. She felt as though she'd never been able to say good-bye to him. My mouth dropped open. "That's what happened to me. My father died unexpectedly of a heart attack when he was fifty. I wasn't with him and my mother didn't have a viewing or an open casket. I never got to see him again or say good-bye. I've always felt like I never truly grieved, and in the ten years since he died, I haven't been able to think about him without crying."

Suddenly, I began to sob uncontrollably, and Diane held me. I later went to the chapel. Sitting there, I sobbed great heaving cries that seemed to come from the depth of my soul. As I cried before God I felt as if my heart would break, but I knew I was releasing ten years of grief.

Eventually, my sobbing subsided. When I looked at my watch, I was surprised to discover I'd been crying for thirty minutes. As I sat there, I wrote my dad a letter expressing my love and gratitude. When I finished it, the healing was complete. God had worked something wonderful inside my spirit. I didn't have to be insecure anymore about my inability to grieve. Since then, I've been able to think and talk about my father without the hurt and pain I experienced before.

Whether or not you need healing in your inner being is something only God can show you. If you do need it, he may lead you to a professional who can guide you through it, or he may speak to your heart right where you are. You can be assured that God's gentle touch will restore whatever you need to continue your walk in security.

Besides experiencing an inner healing, action can also include correcting negative self-talk and analyzing our thinking for incorrect assumptions. We can build our self-esteem by looking at ourselves the way God views us: with love. Putting these tools into action in our lives will strengthen us. We will examine these concepts in more detail in chapter 7.

Earlier we talked about codependency and how it prevents us from growing secure. Here are some principles for breaking that bondage.

• Give up feeling responsible for another person's problem. You don't make him act or feel the way he does.

• Give up thinking you can change that person. You are the only person in the world you can change.

• Give up taking everything personally; it's not your fault. That insecure person is not a reflection of you. The decisions he makes only reflect upon himself.

• Give up looking for your happiness or security in someone else's growth. You can choose to be happy, secure, and contented *right now*, regardless of the problems another person is having.

• Give up thinking all your problems will disappear if the other person will get his life straightened out. You will always experience problems of some sort.

• Give up trying to protect that insecure person from the consequences of his choices. The only way he will change is to experience the result of his actions.

• Give up reacting immediately when someone's need is expressed. Instead, take time to consider whether your natural reaction is really for his "highest good."

Choosing to change in these areas can be the beginning of living free from codependency and insecurity. It will be a process, but you can do it.

As you do, remember these words by Melody Beattie:

It's okay to succeed, to have good things, and to have loving relationships that work. These things may not come easily or naturally. We may struggle and kick and want to hide our heads in the sand along the way. That's okay. That's how growth feels. If it feels too comfortable, too natural, or too easy, we're not growing and we're not doing anything different. We're doing the same things we always have, and that's why it feels so comfortable.[4]

Beattie continues:

A word of caution. From time to time, we may lose our balance. We may start running, skipping, and jumping, then suddenly find ourselves with our noses on the cement. All the old crazy feelings come rushing in. Don't be frightened. This is normal. . . . See it through. Don't be ashamed and don't hide. We can pick ourselves up again. We will get through it. Talk to trusted friends; be patient and gentle with ourselves. Just keep doing the things we know we need to do. It will get better. Don't stop taking care of *us* no matter what happens.[5]

TRUSTING

When we talk about trusting, we have many resources available to us. Resources may include devoting more time to prayer and Bible reading, joining a Bible study, attending church more regularly, and spending time in prayer and fasting.

Donna finds that a half day once a month with God is a soothing experience that builds her security. She sets a full morning aside and takes her Bible, prayer cards, reading material, and journal to a local park. There she spends the time praying, reading, and writing. Often the Lord gives her solutions to problems, reassurance of his love for her, meaningful Bible study time, and other security-building experiences. During this time she can rest, relax, and restore her heavenly perspective of life.

As we grow in our ability to implement spiritual trust, we can also guard our hearts and minds by obeying these commands from Scripture:

Seek first God's kingdom and his righteousness (Matt. 6:33).

Transform and renew our minds to see God's perspective of this world (Rom. 12:2).

Trust in God instead of our own understanding of the way things are (Prov. 3:5, 6).

Take care of our bodies which are temples of the Holy Spirit (1 Cor. 3:16).

Study God's Word, the Bible (2 Tim. 3:16, 17).

Forgive others (Eph. 4:32).

Establishing principles in this chapter firmly in our minds and lives will strengthen and guard us against the opposition that pecks at us. Having a balance between them is very important. If we concentrate only on psychological action or only on spiritual trust, we'll become lopsided rather than well-rounded. We want to take full advantage of both.

As we seek God, he will lead us. He will reveal areas of importance to each one of us in our journeys toward security. Perhaps right now, as you look over the list of options under psychological action and spiritual trust, some items may stand out to you as being of greater need in your life. Start with those, and go from there. Take one step at a time, and trust that when you're ready for it God will lead you in the next step.

PERSEVERING

But what happens when the opposition you are experiencing goes on and on? What should you do when your life doesn't have the "and since I met Jesus, it's been all roses ..." kind of ending (or middle) to it?

Several years ago, I memorized 1 Corinthians 15:58: "Therefore, my beloved brethren, be steadfast, immovable, always abounding in the work of the Lord, knowing that your toil is not in vain in the Lord" (NASB). I was encouraged, but I never stopped to consider what the "therefore" at the beginning of the verse referred to.

Recently, though, I saw that verses 57 and 58 go together: "But thanks be to God, who gives us the victory through our Lord Jesus Christ. Therefore . . . be steadfast. . . ."

That's why and how we can be steadfast: because God will have the final victory! Even if we don't see the end result right now, we can have the faith to know that some day, even it if takes eternity, God will have the victory.

We will examine how to persevere in greater detail in chapter 8, but for now, be assured that God's strength is available to you to endure even in the face of continued opposition.

What opposition to your growth in security have you experienced lately? Have you felt like a chick trying to hatch its way out of a shell, only to be greeted by someone else pecking at you? Take heart. You will make it. With Paul, we can say, "We are hard pressed on every side, but not crushed; perplexed, but not in despair; persecuted, but not abandoned; struck down, but not destroyed" (2 Cor. 4:8, 9).

At the chick-hatching exhibit I told you about earlier, one chick finally pecked a hole big enough in the shell to free himself. All of us cheered his valiant efforts even though he lay there exhausted, wet, and scrawny.

You may feel spiritually and physically drained, but you are working your way free from the fears, bitterness, depression, and negative thinking of insecurity. You are becoming free to experience the security of peace, joy, love, assertiveness, and self-control. Some may "peck" at your efforts, but others cheer for you. I'm one of them. Keep up the good work!

6

...

A Secure Woman Confronts the Sin Around Her

I stood in the jewelry store shifting my weight from one foot to the other as Caron, the store manager, examined my gold bracelet. She finally said, "This is really poor work. Where did you say you had it made?"

"At a store near me," I replied. "I gave the goldsmith an old gold necklace and the diamonds from my great aunt's engagement ring."

Caron wagged her head disgustedly. "I never would have let such bad workmanship leave this store. Do you see the nicks in the gold here and how the soldering shows? I think you should take it back, and make them do it right."

My heart beat wildly at the idea of confronting John—or anyone, for that matter. "I'm afraid I'm not good at that sort of thing. Couldn't you do it over for me?"

"Well, sure, I could, but he should be held accountable."

I gulped hard. Few things were more difficult for me than confrontations. "I'm not very assertive," I mumbled.

Another friend who worked at the store piped up, "Kathy, I'll go with you if you want."

Candie and I agreed to meet at my house the following day and go to John's jewelry store together. Having Candie offer to go with me made me feel braver.

I returned home and told Larry what had happened. Larry knew how difficult it was for me to confront John, who was a Christian. As we talked, I remembered other disturbing things. While I was in Caron's shop, she showed me my "original" design in a standard jewelry brochure. Then, too, John had taken a week longer to finish my bracelet than he promised. Many factors supported the need to confront him, including my anger.

The next day, Candie and I missed one another. "Lord, should I go by myself?" I prayed. Suddenly, I felt God's strengthening, so with sweaty palms, I drove over to the store.

When I walked in, John was helping another customer. I took a seat and mentally prepared my speech, asking God to help me control my nervousness and anger. I wanted to confront him in a godly way.

Ten minutes passed. John excused himself from his customer and turned to me. I had hoped no one else would be around, but I went ahead and pointed out the bracelet's deficiencies and explained exactly what I wanted. Without a word, he wrote up the order and said it would be ready in two weeks. I firmly replied I wanted it on time. With a smug smile, he said it would be.

As I left the shop, though trembling with nervousness, I thanked God for helping me handle the situation in a firm manner.

CONFRONTING ISN'T EASY

Confronting sin or some conflict—in the right way—takes a secure woman. Although I still don't consider myself an assertive person, I've definitely grown in this area. This is a result of becoming more secure in who I am as a Christian and as a person of value.

When faced with the necessity to confront, the insecure woman may think, "I'm not important enough to make an issue over this," or "It doesn't really matter, even if it's important to me." This kind of thinking is basically saying, "I don't have enough value to tell someone else how they've wronged me."

This isn't the way God wants us to think about ourselves. As daughters of the Almightly King, each of us has value and importance. Now this importance is not self-importance; it's the value based on "Christ in me, the hope of glory" (Col. 1:27). And although I have relinquished my rights to God, he doesn't want me to be abused. As God leads, I may need to hold someone accountable if his actions are destructive to me. This doesn't mean I need always to confront. Some silence speaks louder than words. But just as Jesus confronted the money-changers in the temple, he may want me to confront someone.

The book of Nehemiah gives us guidelines for dealing with sin in others. In the fifth chapter, Nehemiah learned that some wealthy men were exacting from their fellow Jews, a practice the Mosaic law forbade.

In his commentary on this passage, Alan Redpath writes,

There are people who were prepared to take advantage of the situation. It must have been very distressing to Nehemiah to find that they were his own people, the Jews. A few were rich, and because they were rich they immediately took the chance to 'feather their nests' at other people's expense, to grant loans at high rates of interest; to make mortgages only under oppressive terms, to take into their homes the sons and daughters of other people as slaves and make it impossible for their parents ever to redeem them again. This whole unhealthy situation led to misunderstanding, trouble, and friction, doubt and suspicion among God's people. Those people who had been so united in objective became divided in affection, and Nehemiah found a situation developing that was threatening to bring to nothing the work of God.[1]

When sin is not confronted in today's Christian community, the work of God can also be brought to nothing. Sin such as gossip, sexual immorality, bitterness, and a multitude of other conflicts divides Christians and destroys the love that should distinguish us as Jesus' servants. When Nehemiah was faced with a problem, he reacted in a godly manner. Nehemiah gives his account: "I was very angry when I had heard their outcry and these words. And I consulted with myself, and contended with the nobles and the rulers and said to them, You are exacting usury, each from his brother! Therefore, I held a great assembly against them" (Neh. 5:6 NASB).

After Nehemiah confronted them, they responded, " 'We will give it back and will require nothing from them; we will do exactly as you say' " (v. 12). Nehemiah received a good result!

Nehemiah's experience points us to some guidelines when we're faced with sin in someone's life or a conflict with others. Nehemiah:

- *coped* with his own anger ("I consulted with myself");
- *confronted* those sinning ("I contended with the nobles and the rulers");
- *communicated* a correction ("I . . . said to them");
- *called* a conference ("I held a great assembly against them").

Let's look at these elements individually and see how we can apply them when we're facing someone's sin or a conflict.

COPING WITH OUR OWN ANGER

When we become aware of a problem, our first reaction may be anger. When this anger first erupts, it is neutral, neither right nor wrong. However, once we become aware of it, we will either cope with it constructively, thereby not sinning, or destructively, thus sinning. As secure women, we want to react in a godly manner that says, "I'm secure in the Lord, therefore, I can respond to my feelings of anger in a righteous way."

Let's look at several concepts that help us react righteously.

Are my expectations unrealistic?

If we're expecting perfection from others or a lack of conflict, we may not be clear why we're really angry. Is my anger because of the other person's sin or because my expectations were unfulfilled?

Ranald Macauley and Jerram Barrs write,

Notice that the commands to forgive and to forbear (as well as many others), assume the sinfulness of others. We should expect each other to be sinful, unpleasant at times, and difficult to live with. That is what it means to be a member of the human race at present. If we expect perfection from others or from ourselves, we will only succeed in not being able to appreciate anything that anyone does, or for that matter anything we do. To expect perfection from any but God is to crush them.[2]

Most of us experience anger in the early days of our marriage because we expect our spouse to be perfect. When I met Larry, I believed I'd found Prince Charming. But after the honeymoon, when his suit of armor began to tarnish, I felt angry and betrayed. How dare he have imperfections and inadequacies! Why didn't he keep his part of the commitments we made to each other? He promised we'd pray and have devotions together, raise a Christian family, and he'd do his part to make a perfect Christian marriage. When I realized our marriage was less than perfect, I was faced with my own unrealistic expectations. Yes, Larry was wrong for not living up to the commitments he made, but I was also wrong to angrily nag, pout, and try to change him.

In her book *Creative Conflict* Joyce Huggett writes,

Conflict is an integral part of all close friendships and of every good marriage. Intimacy breeds conflict. You can't have one without the other. In fact the closer two people become, the more they experience the oneness that was God's intention for married people, the more they open themselves to friction. This is inevitable. After all, they are attempting to fuse two imperfect self-oriented persons: to so unite these two imperfects that they become one flesh.[3]

Let's not allow unrealistic expectations to create anger within us.

Am I taking the sin personally?

Anger can result from believing that the other person chooses to sin because of some imperfection in us—that their sin is a reflection of us. This reasoning leads to the conclusion that we are not worthwhile.

David Augsburger sheds light on this when he writes,

Anger is a demand "that you recognize my worth." When I feel that another person is about to engulf or incorporate me (assuming ownership of me, taking me for granted, using me, absorbing me into his or her life-program), I feel angry.

Actually, I first feel anxious. "Anxiety is a sign that one's self esteem, one's self-regard is endangered," as Harry Stack Sullivan expressed it. When my freedom to be me is threatened, I become anxious, tense, ready for some action.[4]

As a secure woman, I don't have to allow my angry feelings to make me react destructively. I can tell myself, "Yes, I'm angry because what he did wrong makes me feel worthless. But that's a lie. What he did is a reflection of himself, not me. He is responsible for his own sin. If I did influence him in any way, I will take responsibility for that, but he is accountable for his final decision."

A husband's act of adultery or wanting a divorce often causes a wife to feel personally responsible. The fact that he eases his own conscience by blaming her makes it harder. But statements such as "If you'd been a more loving wife, I wouldn't have needed to go outside," or "I don't love you anymore—you've changed," are excuses to blame her and eliminate responsibility for his decision.

The secure woman understands what Maurice Wagner says in *Put It All Together:* "Only attempt to control what you are directly able to be responsible for. Only accept responsibility for what you can control. If there is no specific responsibility, there should be no sense of prerogative."[5]

Am I trying to control others and force them to perform according to my specifications?

My anger could be a result of my frustration because the other person acted against my counsel or advice. Maybe my child disobeyed me, and my anger says, "I want him to be perfect so I'll look good." Maybe a woman I'm discipling makes a poor choice, and my anger says, "Why doesn't she listen to me? I don't want her to struggle like I did as a new Christian." Maybe my husband does something foolish in public, and my anger says, "I've told him a thousand times not to do that. Now everyone will think I'm crazy to have married him."

When I have these reactions, I need to consider the conflict as actually something good. Joyce Huggett writes,

> God uses conflict to hold up a mirror in which we may see ourselves reflected. This mirror does not distort, like the hall of mirrors at a fair. No. It reflects all too accurately the sin-infested me and makes a demand, "This is how I want *you* to change." That is why I make the claim that conflict need not be a foe; it can be a friend in disguise. Conflict is the friend who is ruthless enough to show me how God wants to strip me of my self-centeredness, something that is often painful but necessary if I am to grow in the likeness of the Lord Jesus.[6]

As God shows me my wrong reactions to the sin in another person, he will stretch me to the point where I can reject insecure reactions that say, "I must control other people in order to feel secure. I'm secure when they act the way I want them to, when the people and circumstances around me are the way I need them to be." The secure woman can release other people, so God can work in their lives. This doesn't mean I don't confront them when necessary. It means I don't try to control them.

Am I displacing my anger from the past onto the current situation?

When another person's sin reminds me of a past injustice done to me, my anger is displacement from that past experience. Displacement is transferring an emotion onto the inappropriate person.

A letter from my friend in Iowa explains how this occurs. "It might have appeared I didn't hear you yesterday when you talked about how I mirror my childhood feelings, but I did hear you. You're exactly right; that's what I'm doing. When Rose reacts like that to me, all these childhood feelings surface within me, and sometimes I don't realize it. Yes, what she does is wrong, but my anger isn't so much at her as it is at the past injustices I've experienced.

"I never understood why my grandparents, aunts, uncles, and cousins sat by and watched my parents neglect me. Now when I see someone being mistreated, I feel that if I don't do something, I'm just like my relatives.

"The feeling I get with Rose is like that. My sisters and I were dirty and ragged, and most of the children we grew up with weren't allowed to play with us. Rose has a slightly superior attitude toward me, and I know it's her problem, but it causes me to become angry. My childhood feelings are magnified when she distances herself from me.

"But at least I'm beginning to recognize what's going on and I can see the Lord is helping me cope with all of this in a more constructive way."

My friend is growing in security as God strengthens her to correctly identify the true cause of her anger.

We've just examined four reactions to anger that stem from insecurity. The woman growing in security can identify the real cause of her anger and change attitudes from

—"their sin is unexpected" to "their sin is probable."

—"their sin is my fault" to "I will only take responsibility for my part."

—"their sin is caused by my inadequacy to control them" to "I don't need to control anyone except myself."

—"their sin deserves my anger" to "something from my past is influencing me."

Once the secure woman has done this, her reaction can be one of righteous indignation that says, "God has been hurt by this, and it's his reputation I'm concerned about."

CONFRONTING THE SINNING PERSON

How do we confront the sinning person in a godly way? Ephesians counsels: "Speak truth. . . . Be angry, and yet do not sin; do not let the sun go down on your anger. . . . Let no unwholesome word proceed from your mouth, but only such a word as is good for edification according to the need of the moment, that it may give grace to those who hear. And do not grieve the Holy Spirit of God, by whom you were sealed for the day of redemption. Let all bitterness and wrath and anger and clamor and slander be put away from you, along with malice. And be kind to one another, tender-hearted, forgiving each other, just as God in Christ also has forgiven you" (Eph. 4:25, 26, 29-32 NASB).

A basic foundation for confronting is no name-calling, no screaming, right motives, firm words, wanting the best for the other person, desiring their repentance, no expectations as to a response, and a willingness to forgive. Confronting in a godly manner with strong words of rebuke, while expressing our own sadness, is possible. But if we resort to screaming or name-calling, we've lost our credibility, and our effectiveness to encourage change in another person is diminished. Anytime we yell at another person, he, in a way, controls us and the situation. If we do not maintain our composure, he instinctively knows he's in control.

Some guidelines to consider in preparation for confronting are:

1. *Pick a time when you can have the other person's attention.*

2. *Choose a place with a minimum of distractions.*

3. *Prepare what you'll say in advance.* You may want to write it out and practice it. Or you can give your speech to an objective, trusted person who can evaluate it. First Peter 3:15 says "Always be prepared to give an answer . . . for the hope that you have. But do this with gentleness and respect." While this verse refers to sharing the good news, we can also apply it to our preparation for confronting others.

4. *Eliminate any wrong motives.* Make sure you want to heal the conflict rather than hurt the other person. "All a man's ways seem innocent to him but motives are weighed by the Lord" (Prov. 16:2).

5. *Admit any wrongdoing you contributed to the conflict and how you plan to correct it or make changes in the future.* Matthew 7:5 tells us, "First take the plank out of your own eye, and then you will see clearly to remove the speck from your brother's eye."

6. *Avoid sarcasm, exaggeration, getting off the issue, threatening, acting like a martyr, or attacking the other person's character.* "A gentle answer turns away wrath, but a harsh word stirs up anger" (Prov. 15:1).

7. *Don't use absolutes such as "never," "always," "all the time," "every day," or "constantly."* Remember, "In the same way you judge others, you will be judged" (Matt. 7:2). If we judge others by a perfect standard, we'll fail because we can't meet it, either.

With these guidelines in mind, we can proceed to the confrontation. If the other person's sin is not against us, we can exclusively use "you" messages. For instance, "You are sinning when you live with the man without being married," "You are hurting your body by taking drugs," or "Your reaction to what Angela said was unfair."

Stephanie has used both wrong and right ways to confront others, and as a result, she has experienced both failure and success. Several months ago, she told her cousin, "You shouldn't yell at your children like that." Her cousin replied defensively, "Everybody yells at their kids." Stephanie became angry and said, "Others may do it, but it's still not right. You're hurting Johnny." The issue went unresolved.

Later, Stephanie realized that when she corrected her cousin, her motives were wrong. Rather than going to her cousin with a spirit of love and helpfulness, she wanted to make her feel bad for what she'd done.

In contrast, Stephanie successfully confronted Jamie, a secretary with whom she works, over Jamie's using office supplies for her home business. This time, Stephanie's motives and attitudes were godly as she calmly told Jamie that what she was doing was stealing. If Jamie continued, she'd have no choice but to report her. Stephanie stressed that she cared about Jamie and didn't want to see her fired. She even suggested stores where Jamie could buy office supplies for a discount.

Jamie defended herself on the grounds that "everyone does it. The company can afford it. I don't take much."

Stephanie repeated that it was wrong and that she feared for Jamie's job. Although Jamie walked off in a huff and has been unfriendly ever since, Stephanie knows she did the right thing.

Stephanie used "you" messages effectively. "I" messages, on the other hand, should be used as much as possible when the other person's sin is against us. "I" messages say what my opinion is, what my needs are, and what I would like. For example, "I really need to know when you're going to be late for dinner, so I can have your dinner ready." "I can't allow you to live here if you continue to see another woman." "I feel crushed when I hear those cruel words. The next time I hear them, I'll leave the house."

When we express ourselves, we need to be aware of ten possible negative reactions the other person can have.

- Projection: "It's their (your) fault, not mine."
- Self-condemnation: "Everything is my fault."
- Rationalization: "It's not so bad."
- Displacement: "The real problem is something else."
- Excuses: "I wouldn't do it if. . . ."
- Promises: "I'll never do it again."
- Intellectualization: "I'll talk about it, but don't expect me to change."
- Parading good deeds: "But look at all the other things I've done right."
- Irresponsibility: "That's the way I am."
- Self-pity: "I've just had it bad in life."[7]

When any of these side-tracking techniques occur, we must say, "I'll be glad to talk about that another time, but for right now, we're discussing _____." Then guide the conversation back to the real issue and that person's accountability.

COMMUNICATING A CORRECTION

Although we can't control or change other people, we can offer them a way to correct their sin that we believe is reasonable and attainable. I say "offer" because it's up to them whether or not they receive and incorporate the correction. If they have a solution themselves, that is fine, too.

If we're talking about a critical issue, it may be necessary to involve some consequence in your correction. For example, if we're confronting an alcoholic husband, we may need to communicate that we will separate if there is no change. Or, if we're dealing with an unfaithful husband, we may need to say that we will divorce him if he continues to see the other person.

However, for most insignificant issues, it is best to leave the results to God. That doesn't mean we can't express our needs, but ultimately we must give up our belief that we can change the person. Sometimes we need objective counseling to determine which issues are important enough to take a stand on and which are acceptable to release. If, for example, we're displacing pain from the past, we probably can't judge whether an injustice is significant or not. But whenever we're dealing with "lesser" issues, we must remember that the relationship is more important than the issue.

CALLING A CONFERENCE

If we are dealing with a major issue such as alcoholism, drug addiction, adultery, abuse, or financial mismanagement, we need to involve others by calling a conference.

Matthew 18:15-17 instructs us: "If your brother sins against you, go and show him his fault, just between the two of you. If he listens to you, you have won your brother over. But if he will not listen, take one or two others along, so that every matter may be established by the testimony of two or three witnesses. If he refuses to listen to them, tell it to the church; and if he refuses to listen even to the church, treat him as you would a pagan or a tax gatherer."

If the other person will not admit his problem and seek a solution, we must bring in the assistance of others: another friend, our pastor, a counselor, the police, or other civilian authorities. Holding our unrepentant brother accountable for his reactions and encouraging him to change is the loving thing to do. After we have called a conference, it may be necessary to separate ourselves from him. This may mean divorcing an unfaithful spouse, breaking off a friendship, or refusing to have contact with another person. Such steps should never be taken without much prayer and, if necessary, counsel from Christian professionals.

My friend, Joyce, recently used some of the principles we've discussed to confront a friend about a sin. When she learned that Lynne, a new Christian, was spending weekends at her boyfriend's house, she knew she must confront Lynne. With a trembling spirit, Joyce arranged to have lunch with Lynne, and after some chitchat, asked, "Are you having a physical relationship with Jeff?"

Lynne looked embarrassed, and replied, "Yes."

Joyce then gently shared how Christians are to live differently than the world and how, as a new creature in Christ, she was bought with a price to live a pure life. "You know, I haven't felt right about it," Lynne admitted.

Later, Joyce learned that Lynne had stopped having sex with Jeff. From that point on, Lynne began to grow as a Christian, and Jeff accepted the Lord. A short time later, they married and now attend a Bible study taught by Joyce and her husband.

Joyce reflected on the courage God gave her: "It was successful not because of me, but because of God's leading. Lynne and I recently had an opportunity to talk about what happened and she told me, 'I felt loved when you confronted me.'

"Although that story has a happy ending, another time I confronted a friend about a sin in her life, and she rejected me. But I'm not responsible for the outcome, only for my obedience to God."

WHEN YOU'RE THE GUILTY PARTY

A small article in the December 27, 1988, Los Angeles Times read,

> Firefighters rushing to an emergency left a pot of frying oil on the firehouse stove, resulting in a $10,000 blaze that will close the station at least a week.
>
> The blaze broke out after the six-member squad on Christmas duty received a call to help a rescue team trying to resuscitate a man. . . . The firefighters failed to turn off the burner that was heating oil for frying potatoes.
>
> "We tell people not to do that kind of stuff," Acting Battalion Chief Martin McMahon said Sunday. "We all come from the human race. We make mistakes."[8]

We need to remember the chief's words whenever we are tempted to concentrate on the sins of others. At such times, we need to remind ourselves that we will be the guilty party at times. Are we then going to have the security to confront ourselves and deal with our own sin?

That challenge stared me in the face recently when a friend confronted me about something I had done to hurt her deeply. I was shocked! I wanted to say, "I don't hurt people! All my friends say I'm a wonderful friend!"

Although I replied that I was sad she was hurt, I defended myself, refusing to believe I'd done anything wrong.

When she persisted and told me other unloving reactions I'd had in the past, I felt hurt and attacked. I couldn't believe I'd reacted like she claimed.

Over time, however, as I became more open to the truth, the Lord gently corrected me and helped me see that my friend's comments were valid.

For a time my self-esteem and security sagged. I felt as if I were on the edge of a cliff labeled "Depression." It took all my reserve energy to not fall over that cliff.

I even became paranoid. *My friends really hate me, they're just not telling me,* I told myself. *No wonder Susie hasn't called lately. I remember some things I said the last time I talked to her. She must have misunderstood them. Now she hates me too.* I tried to remember everything I'd said to friends and my reactions.

Trapped in this web of negative self-talk, I felt condemned. *I hurt a friend. How can God still love me? I'm not a very good example.*

For more than a month, I could think of little but this rift with my friend. Occasionally, when I took "captive every thought to make it obedient to Christ" (2 Cor. 10:5) and told myself the truth: that I was still loved and valued by God and a "good" Christian, I experienced relief. But it took tremendous energy to finally believe it and forgive myself for what I'd done.

If Satan can't defeat us through discouragement from someone else's sin, he may try to make our own sin seem so unbelievably bad and unforgivable that we have no hope. The result: powerless living and stunted growth in security.

To fight back, we must remind ourselves of the truth shared by Chief McMahon: "We all come from the human race. We make mistakes."

None of us is exempt from making wrong choices, and just as God wants us to forgive another person, he wants us to forgive ourselves.

In my book, *Healing the Angry Heart*, I wrote about the reasons God wants us to forgive ourselves:

• because we have the right since Jesus already paid the penalty for our sins.

• because then fellowship with God will be restored, and we'll have the power of the Holy Spirit to live the way he wants us to live.

• because it's for God's sake, too. "I, even I, am he who blots out your transgressions, *for my own sake,* and remembers your sins no more" (Isa. 43:25, italics added).

• because it frees us from dwelling upon ourselves so that we can again think about the needs of others.[9]

Looking back on my experience, I don't know why I was so surprised at my sin. After all, am I so perfect that I'll never sin? Obviously, this doesn't mean I try to sin, but only that I'm a sinner saved by a great, gracious God. He's not surprised when I sin and invites me to accept his forgiveness and forgive myself.

I experienced the freedom of knowing I'm forgiven, cleansed, and ready to see how God will restore the relationship with my friend. You can do the same.

As you and I consider whether God is calling us to confront someone's sin or deal with our own, let's keep in mind how we can cope with our own anger, confront the other person in a godly manner, communicate a correction, and if necessary, call a conference.

7
...
A Secure Woman Is Unthreatened by Worldly Thinking

Tears streamed down my cheeks as I sat in the darkened theater watching *The Man of LaMancha*, a play based on Miguel de Cervantes' *Don Quixote*. Long after the death of chivalry, an old man, Don Quixote, set off in a rusty suit of armor to do battle against evil. His goal: to right the unrightable wrongs. He and his companion Sancho arrive at a downtrodden establishment where they are served by Aldonza, a barmaid and prostitute. Because he is capable of unconditional love, Don Quixote sees her as a pure and beautiful maiden. He calls her Dulcinea, and he dignifies her by calling her a "lady" and treating her tenderly.

But Aldonza's self-image is so poor she rejects his image of her. As time passes, Aldonza tells Don Quixote of her background and why she can't think of herself as a lady: she was illegitimate, fathered by "a regiment here for an hour . . . I can't even tell you which side."

When Don Quixote continues to call her "M'lady" and "Dulcinea," she accuses him of cruelty. He has shown her something good that she can't handle.

As I watched the play, my tears made me realize how much I related to Aldonza. Oh, I'd never been a prostitute nor was I illegitimate; I'd never been beaten. But the attitude that caused Aldonza's pain was the same as the one I'd struggled with since childhood. My insecurity and low self-esteem were like hers because I judged myself a failure even though I often succeeded. Because I couldn't be perfect, I felt unlovable and unacceptable to everyone including God.

Becoming a Christian in my late teens helped me understand God's unconditional love for me, but it wasn't until I overcame my abusive reactions to my daughter that I understood my position in Christ. As I watched the play, I heard Don Quixote unconditionally accept Aldonza and speak of her potential. With tears of joy, I silently thanked God that he saw me in the same way. I had discovered God's unconditional love that bolstered my self-esteem and enabled me to experience his security.

Maybe you still feel like Aldonza. You sense God's regarding you as "a secure lady," hear his assurance that you are "forgiven, loved, redeemed, chosen, and blessed," but your past "mental tapes" drown out his tender, loving voice. Maybe like Aldonza you reply to God, "You've shown me what I'm supposed to become, a secure Christian woman, responding in love and dependence on you, but what good is it when it's so impossible for me? Changing takes too long and it is too painful." Then, like Aldonza, you cry, "I am only Aldonza . . . I know that I'm nothing at all."

Sister in Christ, no matter how hopeless your situation seems, you *can* have hope. God is the God of the impossible, and your continuing growth in him will give strength to you and glory to him. He promises that he has begun a good work in you and will carry it to completion until the day of Christ Jesus (Phil. 1:6).

Just as Aldonza was held prisoner by her poor view of herself, the Christian woman can be held captive by insecure worldly thinking. To grow into a secure Christian "lady," she needs to eliminate "I know that I am nothing at all" from her thinking and vocabulary. She needs to break that bondage.

WRONG ASSUMPTIONS ABOUT LIFE

This worldly thinking is the thought patterns within us that contradict who Scripture says we are and what we should be doing as Christians. These thought patterns are based on false assumptions we believe are valid; that is, that life operates in a certain way. Our reactions toward the events in our lives are also conditioned by these often unconscious thoughts. Not that all of our perceptions are wrong, sometimes they *are* biblical, but most of us start out life with more ungodly assumptions than godly ones. When we become Christians, we must continually change our wrong assumptions. They can be corrected by receiving the truth from the Bible and by the instruction of others. Reading God's Word can challenge incorrect assumptions we have and help us change our thought patterns and actions as a result. Paul tells us, "All Scripture is God-breathed and is useful for teaching, rebuking, correcting and training in righteousness" (2 Tim. 3:16).

With God's help, we can also evaluate our thought patterns as we hear others share correct assumptions. This doesn't mean we accept everything other Christians say, but we can use discernment before we accept new ideas, and verify them with mature Christians we respect.

Having the input of other Christians against which we can test our assumptions is one reason for Christian fellowship. "Let us consider how we may spur one another on towards love and good deeds. Let us not give up meeting together, as some are in the habit of doing, but let us encourage one another—and all the more as you see the Day approaching" (Heb. 10:24, 25).

Romans 12:2 talks about this process of adjusting incorrect assumptions. "Do not conform any longer to the pattern of this world, but be transformed by the renewing of your mind. Then you will be able to test and approve what God's will is—his good, pleasing and perfect will." Revising assumptions is part of the process of transforming our minds.

In his book, *Effective Biblical Counseling,* Larry Crabb comments, "Paul says that transformation depends upon renewing our minds. Said in another way, our motivational energy can be channeled in different directions if we change our thinking about what will meet our needs. My efforts to change should not focus on my behavior but rather on my wrong thinking."[1]

Let's look at how our thinking process works:

I have a basic assumption about life

↓

Something happens to me

↓

I experience an emotion based on my assumption

↓

I make a decision to act

↓

As I react to the same thing over and over again, an attitude is formed within me.

For example, Peggy's mother ran a business from her home. Peggy's grandmother cared for Peggy. Whenever Peggy wanted to ask her mother something, her grandmother said, "Don't bother your mother, she's doing something important." As Peggy grew, she heard these words repeatedly, and eventually she formed an assumption about herself: "My needs aren't important enough to bother Mommy. The only time my needs are important is when I have an emergency."

Peggy matured, married, and had children. She was a tireless, selfless Christian wife, mother, and church worker. But whenever she became exhausted, she unconsciously created an emergency so that her valid need would be met.

Through counseling, Peggy saw how her assumption, "My needs aren't important," brought havoc and insecurity into her life. Over time, she changed that wrong assumption to a correct one: "My true needs are important. It's all right for me to express them and look to God to meet them through himself or other people."

Over time Peggy corrected her wrong assumptions: her thinking was transformed in accordance with God's thinking. Now she has freed herself from being a tireless martyr who must do everything asked of her. She has become a secure woman who can say, "No!"

CHANGING ASSUMPTIONS

This process of changing—and living the Christian life—can be compared to driving a car. Driving down the street is not necessarily driving in a straight line. We constantly make minor corrections of the steering wheel so it's usually a crooked one. Maybe the car's alignment is off or the wheel hits a chuckhole or we swerve to avoid hitting a pedestrian. After each incident, we return to the basic direction we're going.

Modifying life assumptions occurs in the same way. As we move along in our thinking by following the Lord, we seem to go straight ahead. But soon we veer to the left because we think, "Why doesn't my husband talk to me and meet my needs instead of reading the newspaper?" In that moment we have a choice. Are we going to continue to follow the wrong assumption: "I'm not important unless my husband talks to me"—a route that leads to bitterness? Or are we going to correct the steering wheel of our minds by saying, "God, you said I'm important to you, and you want me to choose to love my husband and not build up resentment. I'll tell him that I'd like to talk to him after he's finished the newspaper."

In that moment of correcting our wrong assumption and expressing our needs in a godly way, we've transformed our minds to think the way God wants us to think.

Let's look at a few commonly held incorrect assumptions:

It's my right to be happy. Happiness and joy are different. Happiness is a response to circumstances going the way we want them to; joy is an inward response of trusting God regardless of the circumstances. God has promised us joy, not happiness.

My husband (or someone else) should meet my needs. Although God uses people as instruments to meet our needs, ultimately he wants us to look to him. We cannot make someone else fully responsible for meeting our needs.

I shouldn't have to tell my husband (or someone else) what I need. If it's important to me, it should be important to him. This incorrect assumption believes another person can read our minds. Especially when dealing with men, women must understand that God has created the two sexes to be different: what is important to a woman is often not important to a man. Varying temperaments also contribute to our differences. If a sanguine woman, who loves to have fun, is married to a phlegmatic man, who is naturally unmotivated, the sanguine can't expect a party (which is important to her) to be important to her more relaxed husband. Sometimes she will have to sacrifice her own desires even after appropriately expressing her needs.

If I don't say yes to everyone's requests, I'm not God's servant. Even Jesus said no to other people's requests. According to Luke 5:15, 16, "The news about him spread all the more, so that crowds of people came to hear him and to be healed of their sicknesses. But Jesus often withdrew to lonely places and prayed."

The crowds wanted Jesus to meet their needs. But Jesus also had needs, and one of them was to spend time alone with the Father. Jesus made sure his own needs were met, so that he had the energy and power to minister to others.

My child is a reflection of me. The decisions our children make are not reflections of us as parents. Our needs for significance can not be met through the good performance of our children.

I'm responsible to save my loved ones. Psalm 49:7 tells us, "No man can redeem the life of another or give to God a ransom for him." We can influence a person by being the godly woman God wants us to be, but we're not responsible for another person's decision to receive Christ.

I'm not significant if I stay single. A woman's value has nothing to do with whether she's married or single. If you're single, God may have a special goal for you as a single woman. Don't judge your value by whether or not a man loves you.

We've considered a few of the many possible false assumptions that can operate in our lives; now let's consider how Satan uses them to *destroy*, *confuse*, *discourage,* and *promote* mistrust in us.

DESTRUCTION

Satan's first desire is to destroy our commitment to Christ. Perhaps he whispers this wrong assumption in our ear, "God won't keep forgiving you for the same thing." The truth is God puts no restrictions on how many times he'll forgive us. When the Bible says, "If we confess our sins, he is faithful and just and will forgive us our sins and purify us from all unrighteousness" (1 John 1:9), it doesn't add "but don't do it too many times or this promise becomes null and void." No, God's forgiveness is unlimited.

Another false assumption from Satan is that Christians should be perfect. Patty, a new Christian, stopped going to church after her pastor left his wife and two children to run off with another woman. More mature Christians tried to tell Patty that Christians aren't perfect, but Patty wouldn't listen. If Christianity didn't change a person, she didn't want it.

Christianity *does* change a person from death to life, but that life doesn't mean perfection on this earth. Although Satan can't take away the salvation of a person who knows Christ as Savior, he can, unfortunately, succeed in stunting his growth as a Christian. We need to correct these wrong assumptions that can destroy our commitment to Christ.

CONFUSION

If the enemy can't destroy our commitment to Christ, he may try to confuse us. One example of confused thinking is our doing many "good" things but not the "best" things God wants us to do.

If a woman has a false assumption, such as, "If I don't do it, it won't get done," Satan can play upon it by keeping her busy with Christian work but not necessarily the "work" God wants her to do. We must be careful to seek God's voice before we agree to take on a project or job. We would be wise to ask ourselves: *Does this commitment need my spiritual gifts? Does it fit into my priorities and the goals I believe God has for me? Is the timing right? If I don't do the job, what will happen?*

Beware of compulsions. Compulsions say, "I must. . . ." If this sounds like you, see if you can correct your thinking to "Maybe I should. . . ." Once you've reached that step, you may be able to ask, "Must I. . . ?" Next ask yourself, "What would happen if I don't do it, or if I do it at another time?" Don't let ungodly assumptions confuse you so that you don't accomplish God's best in your life.

DISCOURAGEMENT

First cousin to confusion is discouragement. Discouragement often follows disappointment over having our goals blocked, being misunderstood, or seeing our needs go unmet. Incorrect assumptions that contribute to this weakened state include, "If my husband cleans the house, he thinks I'm a messy housekeeper," or "If my mother-in-law offers to take the baby for the weekend, she thinks I'm an incapable mother." Both assumptions presume to know the motives behind a person's actions.

Recently when I spoke to a group of young mothers, I shared these ideas about incorrect assumptions. One woman responded, "My husband comes home from work angry and starts cleaning the house. It makes me so mad because I just know he's thinking I didn't do any work all day long." As I asked her more questions, she finally realized that her husband was working out his own frustrations about his job by cleaning the house. For the first time, she realized that he wasn't criticizing her cleaning skills, but rather was using that activity as a way to vent his anger. Several other women in the group laughingly asked if she rented him out.

Another woman shared how she had viewed her mother's daily phone calls as an attempt to control her. At the end of the session, she said, "Now I understand it's probably her way of showing love and concern. I had assumed there was a negative reason behind her calls."

Our insecurity can make us interpret the decisions and actions of others as criticism of who we are. For example, if I feel inadequate about my cooking abilities on a certain day, and Larry comes home, smells the food, and says, "It's a good thing I didn't invite anyone home with me today," I can easily become defensive and angry. I've assumed he's criticizing me. If instead I choose to be a secure woman and not allow my assumption to discourage me, I can ask him, "Why do you say that?" He may say, "It smells so good, I want to eat it all myself." Now the chances of his complimenting *my* cooking aren't overwhelming, but I can't assume his comment is critical unless he shows me it is.

However, if Larry did reply, "Because I wouldn't want anyone to die with me," I must have the security to say, "It's true I'm not the greatest cook, but I'm trying my best and trust I'll continue to improve. You could encourage me by telling me when I've fixed something you like."

If someone's negative comment makes me feel insecure, I'm depending on that person's approval for my security. I'm operating under the assumption, "I need their approval to be secure."

If a woman believes that her entire reason for living depends upon her husband's love, more effective wifely behavior may help her reach the goal of more attention from her husband, but she will not have added an inch to her spiritual stature. Biblical counseling first should teach her that *Christ* is her reason for living (right thinking), *then* should help her become a better wife (right behavior), not primarily to win her husband, but rather to please the Lord and minister to her husband (right goal). If he loves her in return, praise the Lord. She should enjoy his love thoroughly. If her husband does not return her love, she still is a whole, secure woman, capable of going on for God.[2]

We're often discouraged when we assume we understand what someone else means, rather than ask for more information. Our incorrect assumption is, "I know what they mean, and I don't like it."

After our nine-year-old son Mark was hit twice by pitched balls during a Little League game, he refused to go in to bat again. At home, Larry told him, "If you don't bat next time, you'll never bat again." I furiously assumed he meant he would not allow Mark to play. How dare he stop our son from playing baseball!

When I cooled off, I realized Larry meant, "If you don't bat next time, you'll be too afraid to ever bat again." He wasn't restricting Mark from playing, rather, he was telling Mark that someone who's been hit has a hard time batting again. This incident reminded me once more of the importance of asking questions, such as, "What do you mean by that?" "I don't understand—could you say it another way?" "Do you mean . . . ?"

As you interact with others, be aware of wrong assumptions that can create discouragement.

MISTRUST

Beyond destroying our faith, confusing, and discouraging us, the enemy likes to promote mistrust of God's character. Satan wants to weaken our confidence in God's power and his ability to take care of us in the midst of our struggles and burdens. Satan may trigger an assumption, such as, "Well, I know God can work, but it's impossible for him to help me in this particular situation. Therefore, I'd better take care of it myself."

Of course, God wants us to act in obedience to him, but the action I'm talking about is that of operating without his permission and power. When this happens, my activity is motivated by fear, anxiety, and distrust of God's character, such as when I believe, "God doesn't really love our family enough to give Larry sufficient love for his son."

That's how I felt another time when Larry and I disagreed on how to discipline Mark. I thought we should be sympathetic; Larry thought we should be firm. I thought, *Larry doesn't love Mark enough. I always know what's best for Mark.* Although I sensed my assumptions were wrong, my fear for Mark made it difficult for me to trust God in this case. I wondered if God could really work in this situation.

Suddenly I realized I needed to praise God for our situation because it was an opportunity to see him work. Not feeling very thankful, I began to verbally praise God: "Lord, I don't feel very trusting, but I believe with my will that you are powerful enough to move in my heart and Larry's heart. I surrender my control in this situation and ask you to change our attitudes according to your will."

Within a short time, my heart rejoiced with praise for God, and my feelings followed my decision to trust him. I didn't know how God would work, but I knew I'd done the right thing in releasing control over the situation.

That evening when Larry and I went to bed, he said, "I've been trying to figure out how I can spend more time with Mark." Tears sprang to my eyes as I realized that God had moved in Larry's heart to make him more sensitive to Mark's needs. We talked for at least an hour and reached a compromise of how Larry could sensitively discipline Mark while I would be more firm. We also decided to look for something Mark and Larry could do together. Several months later, Larry took Mark to the driving range, and they discovered their mutual love for golf.

I don't always see such quick, positive responses to my prayers, but even when I don't, I trust God and his characteristics of love and faithfulness. If we concentrate on the times God didn't answer our prayers with a yes or he seemingly didn't do anything in a situation, our distrust of his power can be heightened. At times, God's workings aren't evident, or they take longer than we'd like. To resist such mistrust, we must focus on the times when he *did* answer our prayers the way we asked and *did* change a situation. This kind of remembering will strengthen our trust in him.

Isaiah 50:10 tells us, "Who among you fears the Lord and obeys the word of his servant? Let him who walks in the dark, who has no light, trust in the name of the Lord and rely on his God." This refers to a person who fears and obeys God, but who *also* walks in darkness. At times, we all feel like we're walking without knowledge of what God wants us to do or as if God isn't walking beside us. During these times we need to respond like the pleading father in Mark 9:24, "I do believe; help me overcome my unbelief."

This sincere prayer honestly shares what we're feeling: something God knows anyway. He wants to encourage us to grow in faith by answering our prayers and making a difference in our struggles. In the times of "darkness" we must trust and rely on him even more instead of becoming confused, discouraged, or growing in mistrust.

By the end of the play, Aldonza had made startling changes. Influenced by Don Quixote, she now began to look and act like Dulcinea—a lady. Beginning with Don Quixote's gentle urgings, the transformation became complete as she accepted his evaluation of her. She corrected the wrong assumptions she'd had about herself and began living the truth of who she really could be.

As the strains of the final song of *The Man of LaMancha* were accompanied by the applause of the audience, I felt my tears flow again. After all, hadn't God done the same transformation in my life? He was still lovingly correcting my false assumptions, enabling me to live powerfully in his name—not destroyed, not confused, not discouraged, not mistrusting. To the people around me, my applause may have seemed to join with theirs, but I was applauding my great God for the magnificent work he is doing in my life to make me into his lady—a secure woman.

Have you recently raised your hands in praise to God for the work he's doing in your life? Even if the progress you've made seems minimal, know that he'll continue the process. When you do that, you're on your way to security!

8

· · ·

A Secure Woman
Steadily Perseveres

The telephone rang, and I turned from the keyboard of my computer to answer it.

"Hi, honey. It's Larry. What're you doing?"

"Just revising that article I'm working on. The kids are out playing. How's your day going?"

"Fine. . . ." After a pause, Larry continued, "Kathy, I've got some bad news. I'm going back to night shift with Mondays and Tuesdays off."

I stared straight ahead, not wanting to acknowledge what Larry was saying. Within a few seconds, I mentally reviewed the regular day shift with weekends off that we'd enjoyed for the past seven months: Larry had more time with the kids and we'd had a "normal" household, so unusual for a policeman's family.

"Kathy? Are you there?" Larry's voice filtered through my reflections.

"Yes, I'm here. You're sure about this? No chance it can change?"

"Afraid not. Look, are you okay? I know how much you've liked me being home on a normal schedule."

"I just feel sorta numb. I'll be okay. I guess I've taken our new life for granted, hoping it could go on forever. I guess that's too much to expect, isn't it?" My laugh sounded hollow.

"Yeah, I guess so, honey. Listen, I've got to get back to work, but I'll be home the regular time—Kathy, I'm really sorry. I wish I could do something about it."

"I know. Thanks for caring. Bye, luv."

"Bye."

I sat, staring straight ahead for a minute or so. Tears welled up in my eyes. "Oh, Lord, NO! I thought you were going to reward me with a regular life for once. For sixteen years, I've put up with Larry's odd hours. For sixteen years, I've been a good girl, and I've cooperated. Can't you have a little mercy? I'm so tired of Larry's absence at night and on the weekends. I'm so tired of being father and mother to these kids. I'm so tired of going to family events, to church—everywhere—by myself. I just can't handle it. I don't want to cooperate any more!"

As tears cascaded down my cheeks, despair overwhelmed me, and I continued to sob and cry out to God. Thirty minutes, then an hour passed, and my mind became as dark in its thinking as the room in the early dusk hours. Sitting immobile in my desk chair, I felt as if I were shrinking into the padding, becoming smaller and smaller. I wanted to shrivel up and disappear.

Thoughts of escape seduced my mind. *I'll get in the car*

and just drive until I run out of gas. I don't care what happens to me. Or maybe I'll go to a motel and stay the night. I've got to get away. But my body continued to melt into the chair, too heavy to move.

Is this what a nervous breakdown is like? I wondered. *If it is, then let them just cart me off to the mental hospital. I don't care. I'm sick and tired of cooperating.*

Suddenly a verse I'd memorized popped into my mind. "Therefore, my beloved brethren, be steadfast, immovable, always abounding in the work of the Lord, knowing that your toil is not in vain in the Lord" (1 Cor. 15:58 NASB). *Lord don't remind me of that verse. I don't want to be steadfast or immovable. I want to give up and surrender.*

A second thought surfaced. "Don't you want to be that secure woman who perseveres?" Hot tears burned my face, and I mentally screamed back, "No, I don't care right now!"

Everything within me wanted to escape, to end the pain and the loneliness. But in the small sane place in my mind was knowledge that even if I drove for hours or ran off to a motel, I'd still have to return to reality.

When Larry arrived home from work, I was still in that chair. Taking one look at my swollen eyes, he smiled sympathetically and wrapped his arms around me. I choked back my tears, and mumbled, "If you'd asked me last week whether it would hit me this hard, I'd have said no. I never realized your working days meant this much to me."

Over the next couple of days, I gave myself permission to grieve over the loss of Larry's day shift. At our Bible study group, I honestly shared my feelings of anger at God for not keeping what I'd thought was his promise of a "normal family life." Because the group members didn't condemn me for my feelings and allowed me to express my despair, they helped me immeasurably.

During that week, I changed my assumption of "I deserve having Larry on day shift because I cooperated for sixteen years while he worked the night shift" to "I don't deserve anything good, but because of God's grace, I often experience good things in my life." I also released my expectation of a "normal" family life by reminding myself that our children could still grow up normal even when their father worked night and weekend shifts. And I recommitted myself to being steadfast and immovable in cooperating with God's plan for me.

During the period of disappointment, I wasn't very secure, but the secure woman growing within me is learning to persevere in her walk with the Lord. Perseverance or endurance is "inward strength to withstand stress in order to accomplish God's best."[1]

It takes a lot of stress to make a secure woman give up or give in. But if she does, it isn't long before she snaps back into obedience and cooperation with God's plan. Just as "today's mighty oak is yesterday's little nut that held its ground," so, too, a secure woman is yesterday's insecure woman who learned to persevere.

Let's look first at stresses that can prevent perseverance, and then we'll examine the preventive measures a secure woman can take to lay hold of God's strengthening power.

UNREALISTIC EXPECTATIONS

When I expect circumstances or people to perform in a certain way and those expectations aren't met, it's easy to want to give up. *What's the use of trying?* we think when our world disappoints us. *I might as well not expect anything at all.*

Having unrealistic expectations is often the result of a perfectionistic attitude toward life. Because the perfectionist has an all-or-nothing viewpoint, nothing is valuable or acceptable to her unless it's perfectly done. Such thinking makes a person's expectations higher than anyone or anything can reach.

Homemaker Jean Huff Graham shares her experience of when her unrealistic expectations caused her to give up persevering.

The telephone rang, and I answered with apprehension. A great weariness settled over me as I heard the voice of a friend I had counseled many times. Another crisis, another wave of doubt, another reaching out for answers—I had none.

I was tired of people, their problems and everything involved with ministering to others. For six years I had served as friend, counselor, teacher and discipler to many of the women in my church.

Now I found myself cringing every time the phone rang. My compassion for others had been replaced by cynicism and doubts of my own effectiveness. In other words, I had what is commonly called burnout.

Because I knew that God never wastes any experience, however disagreeable, I knew there was much for me to learn during this time. I decided to stop all attempts to minister for awhile and look for answers to my dilemma.[1]

One she discovered was unrealistic expectations. She continues,

This monster reared three ugly heads. First, there

were the expectations others had of me, some real and some imagined. I also had expectations of others.

These combined to cause a critical spirit within me, lack of confidence in myself, and cynicism toward others. Not liking to disappoint friends or to be misunderstood, I spent much valuable mental energy trying to correct or justify myself.

In the end, trying to be "all things to all men" tied me in an emotional knot and rendered me spiritually useless. I wondered if I would ever want to reach out to others again.[2]

In time, Jean Graham did correct those unrealistic expectations, and so can we.

IMPATIENCE

Have you ever been impatient with your ongoing struggles, even surprised that they are never ending? Peter addresses us when he says, "Dear friends, do not be surprised at the painful trial you are suffering, as though something strange were happening to you. But rejoice that you participate in the sufferings of Christ, so that you may be overjoyed when his glory is revealed" (1 Pet. 4:12, 13).

When we're insecure, we're sometimes "surprised" at how much we must persevere, especially in our American society where everything is "instant": oatmeal in a minute, eye glasses in an hour, rice in five minutes. We forget the value of persevering or waiting for something that is valuable. "It's not fair," we pout.

Today, patience is no longer a virtue. We've all sat impatiently at a traffic light wondering why it takes so long to change. I once timed a traffic light and was surprised to see it go through its cycle within two minutes, rather than the five minutes it seemed. Now waiting at a light doesn't seem as bad because I know it's not forever.

Another way to resist impatience is to realize we may not receive all we want in our lifetime, even when our desires are commendable.

An artist may not see his works gain popularity. Vincent Willem van Gogh, who sold only one painting during his lifetime for thirty dollars, now holds the record for the three most expensive paintings ever sold at an auction. The latest one, "Irises," sold for nearly fifty-four million dollars in 1987.

A mother who perseveres and gives godly training to her children, even though her husband doesn't support her, may not see the result of her efforts. Although Susanna Wesley raised ten children, it wasn't until after her death that two of them, John and Charles, led many people to Christ.

Joseph M. Stowell, president of Moody Institute, reminds us,

> God's work is often long-term. For Abraham and Sarah, it meant being faithful now for results beyond the limits of their earthly existence. God, for reasons best known to himself, usually does not choose to produce instant results in and through our lives. His work is done in an alien domain, in hearts that are often hard, confused, steeped in tradition, fickle, and rebellious. Productivity takes time. Persistence demands the patience to let God do his work in his time. He simply asks us to stick to it.[3]

Persevering to gain security is not an instant procedure, it's a long-term process that includes times of success and failure. The insecure woman tries to grow and in the face of failure, gives up. I receive many letters from readers of my book, *Healing the Angry Heart*, similar to this one:

"Dear Kathy:

I read *Healing the Angry Heart* and put many of the principles into action. Things went fine for a while, but then I returned to my old ways. Why can't I get victory? What's wrong with me?"

I write back to tell them nothing is wrong with them. The changes and successes they're looking for are going to take time and perseverance. They can't expect to read a book and put all the principles into effect the next day. It would be better to concentrate on one main principle at a time and move on to another one only when the first is thoroughly ingrained. Although God can deliver instantaneously, he often makes our deliverance a process of growth.

Even though commercials tell us we can have instant cash for the asking, you and I need to be persistent—in spite of impatience.

WRONG MOTIVES

The insecure woman may operate with wrong motives and easily give up, becoming critical and cynical about life. My own lack of perseverance when I heard of Larry's schedule change pointed out my impure motives. I wanted Larry to work on the day shift because it was better for me and my schedule. I also had the incorrect assumption that God should reward me because I'd "been a good girl in cooperating in the past." Of course, I had some "godly" motives, too—I wanted the children to have more time with Larry and for us to be a close family. But wanting daytime hours for my own needs eroded my perseverance, and my wrong attitudes led to my inability to be secure in whatever God planned for me.

Our motives can seem pure to us but still be misdirected. Proverbs 21:2 warns us, "All a man's ways seem right to him, but the Lord weighs the heart." For instance, I may tell myself because I'm serving God I want to please him, but I may be trying to earn his acceptance through efforts. I may not even realize my motive is wrong. If my constant service continues, and I'm not doing what God wants me to, I can easily burn out and wonder why my wonderful energies for God don't strengthen my ability to persevere.

Singer Zoanne Wilkie experienced this.

Sometimes my mercy runs amuck. Once I met a young woman in dire straits and invited her home to live with us. I wanted to cure all the unhappiness in her life and make her life wonderful.

Before too long, life at our house was awful for everyone as this woman became more and more demanding. I woke up every morning dreading the day.

Finally I went to the Lord and said, "Father, can't I let her go?"

His answer totally surprised me. "I never wanted you to take her in the first place."

I learned that when we do great and generous acts for other people, it has to be because the Lord has led us, not because we want to make them or ourselves wonderful.[4]

James 4:3 tells us, "When you ask, you do not receive, because you ask with the wrong motives, that you may spend what you get on your pleasure." This verse could be paraphrased: "When you ask for security, you don't receive it because you want security for the wrong reasons. You want other people to praise you for it."

As we consider wrong motives as hindrances to perseverance, let's ask God to reveal anything that isn't pleasing to him. We need to remember: "Like a coating of glaze over earthenware are fervent lips with an evil heart" (Prov. 26:23).

EMPOWERED BY SELF

Jesus warns us, "Many will say to me on that day, 'Lord, Lord, did we not prophesy in your name, and in your name drive out demons and perform many miracles?' Then I will tell them plainly, 'I never knew you. Away from me, you evildoers!'" (Matt. 7:22, 23). Even if we do godly things, when we do them in our own power, we're operating independently of God. Such activity will quickly weaken our perseverance.

When we're operating in the Spirit's power we see growing in our lives the fruit of the Spirit: love, joy, peace, patience, kindness, goodness, faithfulness, gentleness, and self control (Gal. 5:22, 23). This doesn't mean we'll be perfect, but we should have a growing strength in these areas as we act and react.

We must also distinguish between feelings and choices. I may not *feel* very loving when I take a depressed friend out for lunch, knowing I'll hear a lot of negative talk. However, I can *choose* to love her by being a sympathetic friend while I help her see her situation from God's perspective. Even though my feelings don't indicate I'm operating in God's power, I actually can be because God judges our choices, not our emotions.

By continually asking for God's empowering, by releasing my own desires, and by not operating in my own strength, I will have greater perseverance.

Now that we've identified some obstacles to perseverance, let's find out how to strengthen it.

RELEASING

To persevere as secure women, we must release unrealistic expectations: those we *think* that God has of us, others have of us, and we have of ourselves. Let's see what we can learn from Martha's example.

In Luke 10:38-42 we find the story of Mary and Martha and their individual responses to Jesus. Mary loved to sit at the feet of Jesus soaking in his every word.

Martha, on the other hand, continued to bustle about in the kitchen, tired and irritated that no one, especially Mary, was helping her. Verse 40 says, "Martha was distracted by all the preparations." Because these two sisters were rich, they certainly had servants. Why didn't Martha delegate more responsibility to them? Perhaps her perfectionism and unrealistic expectations made her feel she must be involved in every step of the preparation. Perhaps Martha was trying to earn Jesus' approval by impressing him with her activity.

Jesus tells her, "Martha, Martha, you are worried and upset about many things, but only one thing is needed. Mary has chosen what is better, and it will not be taken away from her" (Luke 10:41, 42).

Could Jesus be saying to Martha, "I understand your need to be busy and get things done, and I appreciate that. But don't think you must fix ten things for us to eat. Just fix one, then come and join Mary. That way you can be the servant you truly are but also get the spiritual food you need."

I believe Jesus is speaking of balance. He's not saying, "Don't fix us anything," but he is saying, "Fix physical food with a loving attitude, and then come and have some spiritual food."

Many of us are like Martha. At holiday time, we have a

list of twenty-five things to do, thinking they all glorify God, and we end up a nervous wreck. Because we're so busy, neither we nor our families have a chance to enjoy one another's company.

By releasing our perfectionist, all-or-nothing perspective of life, we can gain balance. We can stop thinking, *All or nothing,* and instead think, *This or that.*

I'm improving in this area. The other day for company dinner I intended to serve a hot chicken salad, broccoli salad, homemade bran muffins, fresh string beans, hot cinnamon cider, and my famous no-sugar apple pie. Time grew short, but instead of becoming uptight because I couldn't fix everything I'd planned, I told myself, "Number one, they don't know what I've planned, so they won't know if something's missing; and number two, they are more interested in visiting with Larry and me than eating a fantastic dinner."

As the clock ticked away, so did my menu. I substituted canned corn for fresh beans and rolls from the freezer instead of homemade bran muffins. When our guests arrived, I was able to take off my apron and enjoy their company at a less-than-perfect dinner. They didn't seem to notice.

We can also release trying to control other people, thus escaping frustration, disappointment, and discouragement. Recently, when I asked Larry to come with me to see Darcy in a school play, he said he had other things to do. I felt both sad and angry over his lack of support for our daughter. When I told him that attending the play would be the loving thing to do, he replied that it wasn't the only way he could show his love. This was difficult for me to accept because supporting me in everything I did was my parents' way of expressing their love.

That day I wrote in my journal: "Father, I'm fighting a

wall of bitterness. Your strength to tear down that wall is winning, but I feel sad and upset that Larry doesn't see the importance of this. I'm encouraged, though, to realize that in times past, the wall would be up in a second, and I would be pouting for days after. At least now the wall is not an automatic thing; I have the spiritual and emotional strength to resist.

"It also helps me to review the truth that Larry is responsible for his own actions. I am not his Holy Spirit. He is not a reflection of me. I am a secure woman, not threatened by the actions or decisions of others. I don't have to be insecure, thinking I must force others to be crammed within the box of my desires and expectations. I release this burden to you, Father, and choose joy to replace it because I'll praise you."

Before I left I again expressed my desire that Larry go with me, and when he still refused, I released him to be who he wanted to be, and I could be who I wanted to be. If I'd become bitter, in a sense, I would have allowed him to control me. I chose to be a secure woman instead of a controlled one, and I was able to have a cheerful attitude.

If other people seem to be controlling you, it may be because you can't release the grip their unrealistic or wrong expectations have on you. If you know for sure their desires are not what God wants for you, here are some ways to say no, offered by writer Pat King:

1. *Perfectly valid no.* "I've been out three nights this week. I'm staying home and watching television with the kids." Say it like you mean it.

2. *No-after-saying-yes no.* "I've made a mistake. I shouldn't have committed myself. I'm sorry, I'll have to back out." Hang up the phone, and give a huge sigh of relief.

3. *Five-star no.* (This is my favorite: There's no come-

back for it.) "I'll have to pass it up."

4. *Not-right-now no.* "I've done it in the past, and I'll do it in the future, but I can't do it now."

5. *Polite no.* "I'm sorry, but my schedule doesn't permit me to take on any more obligations this (pick one) week/month/year/decade."

6. *No-way no.* This one is for a teenage son who wants you to call your friends for a ride so he can have the car. Look directly in his eyes, smile, enunciate clearly. "No."

7. *Diplomatic no.* "It was so kind of you to think of me. I'm flattered you asked. I'm sorry I won't be able to do it."

8. *Cowardly no.* Backed into a corner? Feeling low on energy or courage or both? Feeling somewhat desperate? Use this one: "My husband/mother/child doesn't want me to do that."

9. *Absolute no.* "I cannot do this. I don't have the desire, the time, the interest, or the energy. NO. Absolutely not. Never." (Save this one for special occasions.)[5]

If you judge yourself to be an unloving person because you say no to a needy person or cause, just remember that Jesus said no to many needy people, as well (Luke 5:15, 16). If Jesus could say no, so can we.

Another way we can release is to delegate responsibilities just as Jesus delegated service opportunities to his disciples. Thinking we must do everything is the fastest way to weaken our perseverance in ministering effectively. Whether it's delegating chores to the children or letting someone else make the flower arrangements for the mother-daughter tea, we must release ourselves from the expectation that we must do everything and be everything that other people need.

Along with burning ourselves out, we'll discourage others from serving. They'll think, "There's no point for me to help on that committee. Kathy's so particular, I'll never be able to please her." No, I must release my expectations of perfection. The mother-daughter tea is not *my* event: it's the Lord's, and I must involve other people, even if things don't turn out perfectly. Anything I do belongs to God; my responsibility is to do what he wants me to do, not be accountable for the result.

BEING EMPOWERED BY GOD

To prevent burnout, we must rely on God's power to operate in our lives. My friend, Lynn, wrote about a time she had to choose to be empowered by God. "Last Tuesday I woke up and was so consumed by anger over the possibility of losing our house in foreclosure that I felt strangled. I was sick to my stomach all day. When I realized I wasn't coming down with the flu, but that I was angry, I asked God to hold me and fill me with more of his love.

"The next day I read the entire book of Job and was reminded of what God has said to me many times: 'Give me the steering wheel of your life (give me control).' When God turns the steering wheel over to my husband, I panic. I know he'll crash. God says to me: 'Will you trust me enough to teach him to drive?' This has been a very useful illustration to me in redefining who is in control over things I cannot change or do anything about.

"Unless a woman reads God's Word, gets to know God, and believes that God is able, security cannot become a reality in her life. What a difference that makes! After returning the steering wheel to God and soaking up his Word, I felt restored to wholeness. It does work."

Lynn is growing in her security in the Lord as she relies upon him to help her persevere even in the midst of great stress.

Being empowered by the Holy Spirit doesn't mean

127

inactivity, however. Lynn will still need to communicate her needs to her husband. Daniel 11:32 says, "but the [women] who know their God will display strength and take action" (NASB). Choosing God's power means knowing who he is and what he wants me to do—then doing it.

CELEBRATING

Have you ever wondered why God told the Israelites to have feast days and festival celebrations? Doesn't it seem a little frivolous? If our view of God is a tyrant who is "all work and no play," celebrations may seem uncharacteristic of him. But such a view of him is incorrect. God's idea of renewal extends back to creation when he rested on the seventh day. Renewal is evident throughout the Bible as God directs the Israelites to allow the land to rest in the seventh year and instructs them to have festivals. Renewal is contained in the fourth commandment to keep the Sabbath day holy, and Jesus completes it with resting and relaxation himself.

Edwin R. Roberts of Princeton Seminary once sat under a pastor who concluded his announcements: "I am not going to take a vacation this summer; the devil never does!"

Roberts went home and re-read the Gospels to see what Jesus' attitude is. He found that of His three years active ministry, there were mentioned 10 periods of retirement! This was in addition to the nightly rest and the sabbath rest.

Whose example are we following? The Devil's?[6]

God's attitude toward relaxation and celebration must influence how we treat our bodies. The secure woman isn't afraid to take time off, whether it's a two-week vacation, relaxing in the evenings, taking a nap, or setting aside time to read a book. For many of us who were raised with the idea that a woman's work is never done, we may feel guilty when we sit down and do nothing. Yet our bodies need time to renew themselves. Being a workaholic, even in God's service, doesn't honor him if our bodies break down from inadequate rest.

One author analyzes what a woman, particularly a mother, needs:

Mothers: How to Keep Them Running Smoothly

Perhaps mothers should come with a maintenance agreement which provides for a complete overhaul every five years, three kids, or 300,000 miles, whichever comes first.

Here are several points which ought to be included:

FUEL: While most mothers will run indefinitely on hot coffee, pizza, and hamburgers, an occasional gourmet meal for two in elegant surroundings will add immeasurably to increased efficiency.

MOTOR: A mother's motor is probably one of the most dependable anywhere. A mother can start and reach top speed from a prone position at a single cry from a sleeping child. To keep that motor at peak efficiency, regular breaks are recommended. A leisurely bath and nap every 1,000 miles, a babysitter every 10,000 miles, and a two-week, live-in sitter every 100,000 miles will do wonders.

BATTERY: Batteries should be recharge regularly. Roses, candy, or other thoughtful and unexpected gifts often do the trick.

CARBURETOR: When a mother's carburetor

floods, it should be treated immediately with Kleenex and a soft shoulder.

BRAKES: Use brakes often. Slow to a full stop regularly.

CHASSIS: A mother operates best when her chassis is properly maintained. Her wardrobe should be changed as needed every fall and spring. Regular exercise should be encouraged and provided for. A complete change of hairdo and makeup should be a part of the regular maintenance. When the chassis begins to sag, there are a number of possible remedies, including exercise and weight loss.

TUNE-UPS: Mothers need regular tune-ups. Compliments are both the cheapest and most appreciated.

By following these simple instructions, the average mother should last a lifetime, providing love and caring to those who need her most.[9]

Whether or not you're a mother, these wise instructions apply to you. And whether or not you're running strong with perseverance or feeling faint and ready to give up, take heed to release unrealistic expectations, operate in God's power, and take time to celebrate. Putting these three principles into practice will strengthen you to be that secure woman who perseveres.

My own ability to persevere was strengthened by the experience of Larry's going back to night shift. Less than a year later, he had a new position that put him back on days with weekends off. I know now not to put my expectation on his schedule; it may change again. But I'm sure going to enjoy it while it lasts!

9
...

A Secure Woman Is Strengthened During Times of Failure

Five minutes before eleven-year-old Mark left for school, we put the finishing touches on his art project about Connecticut. I knew he felt uptight. I was worried, too, wondering if we'd included everything.

After I'd kissed him good-bye and returned to the family room, I looked again at the project's assignment sheet. A light bulb turned on in my brain, and I realized we'd forgotten several things. *How could I be so stupid?* I berated myself. *Kathy, you're a failure as a mother. Now he's going to get a terrible grade!*

I shuffled down the hallway in my robe and slippers. Having a cold didn't help my attitude. My brain felt numb, and my voice was raspy. *How am I going to speak at that women's group on Saturday? I'm trying to trust you, Lord.*

I finished my hair and makeup in front of the bathroom mirror. I disliked my hair style and my face seemed to have sprouted a few new wrinkles. I couldn't believe how bad I looked.

The phone rang and I answered it to hear Larry's voice.

We talked awhile, and before hanging up, he reminded me to get an emissions test done on the car. Later, I drove our Blazer over to the "smog-check" place.

As I sat in the waiting room, I felt better about myself. After all, hadn't I found the repair shop and confidently asked for what I wanted?

After twenty minutes, the mechanic was finished and asked me to sign the form. "By the way," he said, "this is the wrong car for this form. Do you have the right one?"

I stared at him. The wrong car? I glanced at the license plate number on the smog check form and realized it was for our Honda. *Oh, no! I brought the wrong car.*

Disgusted with myself, I paid the man and said I'd be back in a few minutes with the right car.

Driving home, I mused, *Kathy, you've really proven yourself a failure today.*

Failures, big and small, enter our lives in many ways. Maybe we forgot to buy an item at the store, or we said something foolish to someone. Maybe we didn't complete all the items on our to-do list or received a "D" on a college exam. Maybe we misplaced an item at work or didn't read our Bibles. We may have committed adultery or hurt someone in an auto accident.

A sense of failure prevails when we don't succeed in reaching a goal we've set or a desire remains unfulfilled. We also consider it failure if we are unable to perform at the level we expected.

Our sense of failure is subjective. What I may consider a failure, you may consider a tremendous success. While I see only what I didn't accomplish, you may focus on what was achieved and feel good about yourself.

Scripture is clear about behaviors and attitudes that are sinful and therefore failures, such as immorality, lying, pride, and deception. These sins, or failures, aren't what I'm talking about here. Instead, I want to point out that our guilt over many things may not be based on truth.

Former President Dwight D. Eisenhower once said, "When I was a small boy in Kansas, a friend of mine and I went fishing and as we sat there in the warmth of a summer afternoon on a river bank, we talked about what we wanted to do when we grew up. I told him that I wanted to be a real major league baseball player, a genuine professional like Honus Wagner. My friend said that he'd like to be president of the United States. Neither of us got our wish."

If Eisenhower had looked at his boyhood goal in the wrong perspective, he could have considered himself a failure. Yet we know he wasn't.

Whether we consider ourselves failures or successes often depends on our perspective and focus. At times, we set ourselves up for failure with our own unrealistic expectations. If I set a goal to never become angry with my child, I'll consider myself a failure whenever I become angry. On the other hand, if I acknowledge that potential for anger and set my sights on raising my child into a well-adjusted adult, I will most likely succeed and not experience a false sense of failure.

Often what we consider failure may be the groundwork for future success. "Thomas Edison was taunted by some wag before he had successfully invented the incandescent light bulb, 'Ten thousand experiments and you haven't learned a thing.'

" 'You're wrong,' responded Edison, 'I've learned ten

thousand ways not to invent the incandescent electric light.' "[1]

Many times I've felt like a failure in my responses as a mother, wife, friend, or Christian. Often, my guilt and pain over failing was abnormally great in comparison to what I'd done. Unable to view the situation realistically, I would magnify my wrongdoing.

This often happens when we evaluate ourselves according to another person's values or opinions. Herbert Bayard Swope said, "I cannot give you the formula for success, but I can give you the formula for failure: Try to please everybody."[2]

Failure is humanity's common denominator. Yet the secure woman is strengthened in spite of repeated failures and rises to try again. Proverbs 24:16 says, "For though a righteous man falls seven times, he rises again, but the wicked are brought down by calamity." Insecure women may have a hard time "rising again," but our goal as secure women is to forgive ourselves and go forward in God's strength. Kenneth M. Meyer has said, "Failure is God's stepping stone toward a second chance."

The Bible gives us many examples of people who failed and yet received God's strength for future success. Aren't you glad their stories are included in the Bible? If scripture didn't mention Adam and Eve's disobedience, Moses' disbelief, or King David's immorality, but talked only of their obedience, I'd feel discouraged. I'd reason, *There's no hope for me. All the people in the Bible were perfect and I'm not, so I guess God can't love me.*

Isn't it wonderful we don't have to feel this way? God made sure the Bible honestly reflected his forgiveness for man's failures. And because "everything that was written in the past was written to teach us, so that through endurance and the encouragement of the Scriptures we might have hope" (Rom. 15:4), we know God wants us to benefit from the biblical stories of those who failed.

Let's look at some of them and see what we can glean.

ADAM AND EVE

Adam and Eve were given the perfect environment, and yet they failed. Eve's doubt and failure started when she listened to the serpent *question* God's command by saying, "Did God really say, 'You must not eat from any tree in the garden?' " (Gen. 3:1). Then Eve grew closer to failure by *changing* God's message. Eve replied, "God did say, 'You must not eat fruit from the tree that is in the middle of the garden, and you must not *touch it*, or you will die'" (Gen. 3:3 italics mine). If we look at Genesis 2:17 when God gave his original instructions, we find that he didn't mention anything about touching the tree, only about eating the fruit. Eve embellished God's command.

In Genesis 3:4, 5, the serpent *challenged* God's wisdom. "You will not surely die! For God knows that when you eat of it your eyes will be opened, and you will be like God, knowing good and evil." Satan was suggesting that God wanted to withhold something good from Eve, a third step leading to doubt.

Finally, "When the woman saw that the fruit of the tree was good for food, pleasing to the eye, and also desirable for gaining wisdom, she took some and ate it. She also gave some to her husband who was with her, and he ate it. Then the eyes of both of them were opened, and they realized that they were naked; so they sewed fig leaves together and made coverings for themselves" (Gen. 3:6, 7). Once Adam and Eve sinned, they reached the final step of doubt: the great *cover-up*. They became self-conscious, instead of God-conscious, and tried to hide from God (v. 8).

Eve believed Satan's lie: "God is actually withholding

something good from you. He doesn't want what's right for you." She doubted that God wanted the best for her and Adam.

Eleven years ago, I sensed God indicating that a high sugar intake wasn't good for me. Whenever I ate a lot of sugar, I became easily angered and had less energy. But how could I resist desserts when I was a bonafide chocoholic? *God wouldn't ask me to do such a thing,* I reasoned. *He's trying to withhold something from me.*

In time, the connection between my sugar intake and angry reactions became clearer. Still I couldn't resist sweets and felt like a failure. Why couldn't I obey God?

Years passed. Finally, I decided to go off sugar for a week. I couldn't do it. I tried again and barely made it. At the end of the week, I breathed a sigh of relief and pigged out! Of course, I felt guilty again.

The past three to four years, I've increased my times of "freedom from sugar" to the point where I've had very little sugar in the past seven months. My assumption has changed from "I shouldn't be deprived of sugar" to "Eating sugar deprives me of patience, energy, and obedience." I no longer feel like a failure in this area because I've gained control through the power of the Spirit. With more patience and energy, I have no doubt now that God had the best in mind for me. (I want to clarify, however, that I'm not telling other people to stay off sugar, only that it's best for me to do so.)

Once we realize we don't need to doubt God's good intentions for us, we can understand his wonderful plan to take care of failure. As he responded to Adam and Eve's sin, God provided "garments of skin" (Gen. 3:21) far superior to the fig leaves they had made. But he also supplied a long-range solution: "And I will put enmity between you [the serpent] and the woman, and between your offspring and hers; he will crush your head, and you will strike his heel" (Gen. 3:15). The solution? The coming of Jesus Christ to make possible the forgiveness of any and every sin. Yes, Adam and Eve failed and sinned, but in his love God provided a solution (even though they still had to suffer the consequences of their sin).

We learn from Adam and Eve's failure that we don't need to doubt that God wants the best for us. And if we do fail, he forgives us. There is always hope.

MOSES

Exodus tells the story of Moses, a man who disbelieved and experienced failure many times. He had a hard time believing God could work out his plan in his own way and timing. We first see this flaw in Moses when he killed an Egyptian who had beaten an Israelite. Moses' motive was good: he wanted his brothers freed from their oppressors, the Egyptians. Unfortunately, he used his own plan to settle the matter, and when he was found out, he fled to the wilderness.

Forty years later, Moses encountered the burning bush (Ex. 3) and his disbelief again expressed itself. When God commissioned him to free the Israelites, he questioned, "Who am I?" (Ex. 3:11) And then, "What if they do not believe me or listen?" (Ex. 4:1). "I am slow of speech and tongue" (Ex. 4:10). And finally, "O Lord, please send someone else to do it" (Ex. 4:13). Moses couldn't believe God could use a shepherd like himself to deliver the Israelites from the Egyptians.

Moses believed one of Satan's most potent lies: "God only uses perfect people." We need to make sure we don't believe that or other lies such as,

• God is tired of hearing me repeatedly ask for forgiveness for the same thing.

• I'll confess this sin later when I'm living more victoriously.

• I'll confess all my sins at the end of the day before I go to sleep.

• I'm not forgiven unless I *feel* forgiven.

• I should give up trying; I'll never get victory over this.

Such negative self-talk constantly makes us judge ourselves guilty as David Augsburger writes in *Caring Enough to Confront.*

"Wake up," your conscience commands. "It's time to be in court."

"Right, your honor," you reply. Your conscience acts as judge when you're alone. But once downstairs, your wife will occupy the bench. Then, at work, the boss will pick up the gavel. At lunch, Charlie will preside while you tell him about last night's problem with the neighbor who backed over your son's bike. Then, tonight, at home, your brother-in-law Pete (they're coming over for supper, remember?) will be presiding behind the desk.

And you? You're in the docket. On trial. Permanently. One judge follows another. The evidence is heard. You testify—often against yourself. The sentence is passed—"guilty," or "not guilty." And your case is passed on to the next judge.

You know the feeling?

The feeling of being constantly on trial?

The feeling that life is not a stage—but a courtroom? That others have been appointed to judge? And you? You're the judged. Always on trial.

And you put yourself there on the stand, in the stocks, or at the gallows with the noose around your neck.

You are handing out gavels.
You can quit.[3]

Yes, as secure women, we can stop letting other people tell us if we've failed and look to God for an accurate assessment. We can also quit condemning ourselves for our failures and stop doubting that God is strong enough to give us victory. It will require changing our thinking from negative self-talk to believing what God says based on Scripture.

"I, even I, am he who blots out your transgressions, for my own sake, and remembers your sins no more" (Isa. 43:25). God not only wants to forgive us for our benefit, but for his benefit too. He wants delightful fellowship with us.

"For as high as the heavens are above the earth, so great is his love for those who fear him; as far as the east is from the west, so far has he removed our transgressions from us" (Ps. 103:11, 12). When you say, "Lord, I did it again," he replies, "Oh, did you do it before? Well, I must have forgiven you because I don't remember it." He forgets when he forgives.

"The one who is in you is greater than the one who is in the world" (1 John 4:4). God is strong enough to help us overcome any struggle or conflict.

Meditating on verses like these will help strengthen our belief in God's power and unlimited forgiveness.

DAVID

In 2 Samuel 11, we read about King David's failure: wasteful indulgence in pleasure. Instead of going to battle as he should have, he slacked off in Jerusalem and committed adultery with Bathsheba. Then he had her husband Uriah murdered. Yet, God forgives even our "great" sins.

Of course, David suffered the consequences, but he knew God had forgiven him.

Psalm 51 shows David's thoughts: "Wash away all my iniquity and cleanse me from my sin. . . . Create in me a pure heart, O God, and renew a steadfast spirit within me. Do not cast me from your presence or take your Holy Spirit from me. Restore to me the joy of your salvation and grant me a willing spirit to sustain me" (Ps. 51:2, 10-12). David was forgiven and once again experienced the joy of fellowship with God.

Unlike David, many people who have failed through adultery or murder may not rediscover the joy of fellowship with God immediately because they believe their sin is too great for him to forgive.

Yesterday, as I was interviewed on a call-in radio program, a tearful woman called in to ask how she could forgive her husband and herself for their affairs. Of course, there are no easy answers for such problems. The process will be a long one of discovering the underlying causes of their troubled relationship and re-establishing trust. But the radio host and I assured her it was possible. We encouraged her to get the counseling she needed.

Perhaps you have something in your life that seems impossible for God to forgive. It may not be immorality or murder, but in your perfectionist thinking, you can't believe that God still loves you.

Let me assure you that God's forgiveness is for any sin, no matter how bad it seems. Charles G. Ward, director of telephone counseling centers for the Billy Graham Evangelistic Association writes,

We must rest confidently in the finished work of Christ which covers all our sins. We are delivered from the power of sin. As we trust the Lord, though we slip into sin, sin will never again be our master. Some day we will be delivered from the presence of sin as he takes us up and away from this present evil world to be with himself. . . . God delights in extending his forgiveness to the Christian who will ask for it. Even though plagued by the nagging recurrence of sin, we should not despair. He is willing to forgive again and again.[4]

God's promise to you is, "Though your sins are like scarlet, they shall be white as snow; though they are red as crimson, they shall be like wool" (Isa. 1:18).

If it seems as though your failures are scarlet with sin, then take heart. We learn from David that no failure is beyond God's ability to forgive.

ELIJAH

In 1 Kings 19, God's prophet Elijah experienced the most successful incident of his life. He called fire down from heaven to burn up an altar soaked by water. Immediately afterward, Queen Jezebel threatened Elijah, and he ran for his life, becoming depressed and angry. God sent an angel to say to Elijah, "God sent me to tell you to get up from here, get your act together, and stop feeling sorry for yourself. God won't love you again until you're no longer depressed."

Stop! You know, I can't find those last statements in my Bible. The account *actually* says that the angel gave Elijah something to eat and gently encouraged him. Then God personally talked to Elijah, asking him questions and giving him an opportunity to talk about his feelings. God didn't rebuke Elijah for his honest sharing but instead revealed his own presence in a gentle blowing wind. Then God gave him a fresh purpose for living with a new

141

assignment and a new friend, Elisha.

When we're depressed or consider ourselves failures, we may think God is standing in heaven, tapping his foot, arms folded, a scowl on his face. We may think we hear him say, "Now, when are you going to get your act together and shape up? I don't love you anymore because you're a failure."

Because of Elijah's experience, we know this is not true. God actually wants to offer us everything we need to climb up out of our depression and face life with joy again.

Depression has many possible causes:

• anger turned inward

• a false sense of guilt because you were physically or sexually abused as a child

• verbal harassment as a child

• a physical problem.

Whatever the sources of your depression or failure, God doesn't condemn you. He offers you all the help you need. We know this because of Elijah's experience.

PETER

In Matthew, Jesus warned Peter that he would deny him. Peter, of course, couldn't believe he'd do such a thing, yet he did and "went outside and wept bitterly" (Matt. 26:75). Even after Jesus rose from the dead, Peter still felt hopeless and returned to fishing. His negative self-talk may have been, *Even if Jesus is alive, there's no hope for me. I denied him. He said many times that if anyone denied him before men, he would deny him before his Father in heaven. He can't possibly forgive me.* Can you feel his despair?

Then in John 21, Jesus told the disciples to cast their nets into the water even though they had caught nothing all night long. After they did, the great load of fish almost broke the nets.

The atmosphere must have been tense as Jesus and the disciples sat together having breakfast a short time later. Peter's self-condemnation dissolved all remembrance of Jesus' compassion and love, and he may have been thinking, *I wonder when he's going to rebuke me for my failure.*

Instead, Jesus communicated his forgiveness by asking Peter three times, "Do you love me?" Each time Peter replied, "Yes, you know I love you." Theologians tell us Peter's word for *love* was a more shallow word than the word Jesus had used. Perhaps Peter wasn't convinced he loved Jesus as much as he should. Even so, Jesus showed his forgiveness by giving Peter an assignment: "Feed my sheep." Jesus knew Peter would be a strong leader when empowered by the Holy Spirit.

Just as Peter struggled to accept Jesus' forgiveness and to forgive himself, so may we. Sometimes we can accept God's forgiveness more readily than we forgive ourselves. We may think we need to "pay penance" for our failure as if earning enough points will take us off the hook labeled guilty.

My friend Allison abused her son for several years when she was severely depressed. Now he is sixteen and all his problems seem like her fault. Even though she often feels happy about the changes God has worked in her life, she can't let herself enjoy that happiness when her son is around. She recently told me, "How can I be happy in front of Brent when he's so miserable, and I'm the cause of it?"

I reminded Allison she has been forgiven for the past and how detrimental it is for her to continue condemning herself. Rehashing the past and not forgiving herself only blocks her from experiencing God's fullness. And yes, some of her son's problems may stem from the past abuse, but he could also be having these teenage problems even if she hadn't abused him. I encouraged her to believe God could heal her son through his own process of growth.

Then I explained, "The other day, I went to a local park with the six quarters needed to get through the automatic gate. I put in the coins and turned to watch the arm of the gate go up. Only there wasn't an arm. For some reason, it had been taken off and I hadn't noticed it. I suddenly realized I'd paid for nothing. I could have gone into the park for free. Allison, that's what you're doing. You're paying for your past sins when Jesus has already paid the penalty for them. You're entitled to go forward into a park of divine provision without paying, but you keep putting in the coins of self-condemnation. Accept God's forgiveness and then forgive yourself. Every time Satan mentions your past, rebuke him and remind yourself that God has forgiven you."

We learn from Peter that we don't need to condemn ourselves for our failures. We can accept God's forgiveness and forgive ourselves. Then God will show us the sheep he wants us to feed—those people around us who need to know how we've grown as secure women.

Have you ever noticed when the saints from the Old Testament are mentioned in the New Testament, most of their failures aren't mentioned? In fact, God's memory of them seems selective. He records more of their successes and faith in him than their failures. That's not a mistake. God's forgiveness in action is forgiving, forgetting, and remembering our successes in following him.

As you grow as a secure woman, the same thing can happen to you. Here are some suggestions for getting closer to your goal.

Ask God to forgive your failure. First John 1:9 tells us, "If we confess our sins, he is faithful and just and will forgive us our sins and purify us from all unrighteousness." God doesn't forgive us because we deserve it, but because he is faithful and just. He *wants* to do it, so we'll have his power to resist the next temptation.

Forgive yourself. Refusing to punish yourself will free you to take hold of the power God offers you. Let yourself off the hook—God already has.

> Generally, we feel guilt when we do not forgive ourselves for the things that God has already forgiven. We say to ourselves like a broken record, "Why did I do that?" We play "if only" games, and hold a bitter grudge against ourselves.
>
> When you die and see the Lord, and say, "Oh Lord, do you remember that sin?" He will reply "No—what sin?" He promises, "I will forgive their wickedness and will remember their sins no more" (Jer. 31:34). What God has forgiven, he has forgotten; what he has forgotten we need not remember.[5]

Believe that God can use this failure for good. Romans 8:28 applies even to failures. God can turn anything into value if we'll let him. Peter's denial is testimony to that. It tempered his dependence on himself and helped him become a leader sensitive to the Spirit.

When Satan reminds you of the past, rebuke him in Jesus' name. Turn your negative self-talk from "I'm still guilty" to "God has forgiven me and I'm free." You may have to do this many times, but eventually, the false guilt will diminish.

"When you begin to think about past sins, beware of letting your feelings dictate what is truth. Rather, allow truth to dictate your feelings. Turn to your Bible and read again God's promise of forgiveness in 1 John 1:9. Remind yourself that this—not your feelings—states the truth, and then believe it. Start saying, " 'Thank you for forgiving that particular sin, Lord.' "[6]

Ask God to use your failure to glorify his name. Second Corinthians 1:3, 4 tells us, "Praise be to the God and Father of our Lord Jesus Christ, the Father of compassion and the God of all comfort, who comforts us in all our troubles, so that we can comfort those in any trouble with the comfort we ourselves have received from God." As you minister to the needs of others with the same help God gave you, he will be glorified.

For many years, a small ceramic cup sat in a place of honor on my piano. My great aunt had made it for me and painted my name on it when I was born. Some time ago, Mark and a friend kicked a soccer ball onto the piano and broke the cup. Looking at the broken pieces on the tile floor, I sadly wondered if I could glue them back together. As I bonded the pieces together, tears filled my eyes.

How silly to be so sentimental, I chided myself, *but this old cup really means a lot to me. I want to hand it down to my grandchildren.*

When I finished, tiny particles too small to be glued lay on the table. Tears tumbled down my cheeks as I inspected the repaired cup. My name was intact, but the cracks and odd-shaped holes made it obvious the cup had been glued. *Maybe if I position it just right, people won't notice the cracks from a distance.*

I gently placed the cup back on the piano. Stepping back to look at it, I was surprised to feel prouder of it than ever before. My efforts to repair it showed how much I loved it.

Then it hit me. That's how God feels about us when he

forgives our failures and restores our hope and joy. Some cracks and small holes of imperfection may be left in our lives, but we are still treasures to him; treasures he spent time and effort healing back together with the glue of his Holy Spirit. And we are living examples of his love.

I took one last look at the cup before returning to my housework. *That cup will never be whole again,* I said to myself, *but forgiven lives will be completely healed one of these days in heaven—even those who have failed.*

10

...

A Secure Woman Lives a Powerful, Godly Life

While we were on a skiing trip, our home area was the victim of strong winds. A few days later when I visited our neighbors Hank and Bernice, Hank asked, "Did you notice that those high winds knocked over our tree in back?"

"I'm really surprised." It looked so healthy and strong.

Bernice responded, "We were surprised, too, because it didn't seem diseased. But when the man came out to haul it away, he called it a 'dumb tree.' "

I stared at her. " 'Dumb tree?' What did he mean?"

Hank continued, "He told us it was a dumb tree because it didn't send its roots deep into the soil. Even though it had been there many years, its roots weren't deep enough to support its full height, and the wind yanked the roots right out of the ground."

As we talked, I remembered hearing about another tree in a Colorado city square that everyone admired, not knowing it was diseased. One day without warning, it fell to the ground, exposing its rotten roots.

These two trees, one with shallow roots and the other with rotten roots, remind me of women who outwardly appear secure and godly, but whose hearts have shallow commitments to Christ. They may even harbor long-term unconfessed sin. Eventually, their inner beings will be exposed.

That was what happened to Jackie. She and her husband Chris were active in their church and appeared to be growing in Christ. Then rumors circulated until a friend confronted them, "Are you involved in pornography?" They admitted they were. Jackie said she cooperated with her husband's desire for it but wanted to stop.

Even though Chris destroyed most of his pornographic films, he kept some magazines and eventually began an affair with another woman. Devastated, Jackie felt she couldn't depend on the Lord for the security she needed. She filed for divorce and began to date unbelievers who spent weekends at her home.

As women growing in security, we don't want something like this to happen to us. Instead, we want a deep walk with Christ "firmly rooted and now being built up in Him and established in ... faith ... overflowing with gratitude" (Col. 2:7 NASB). We also want an inner spiritual life free from unconfessed sin. Although we'll never be permanently free from sin in this world, we do want to become aware of both temptation and unconfessed sin in our lives.

In this chapter, we'll examine three aspects of keeping our roots in Christ healthy and strong: recognizing temptation, taking a look inside ourselves, and staying committed to Christ.

TEMPTATION

D.L. Moody said, "When Christians find themselves exposed to temptation they should pray to God to uphold them, and when they are tempted they should not be discouraged. It is not a sin to be tempted; the sin is to fall into temptation."[1]

Temptation is not sin; giving into it is. This is an important concept for us to remember.

How can temptation sway us toward sin? Let's look to Proverbs 7:10-23 for the answer. In this passage, we see temptation in the role of an adulterous woman. The things she does to entice an unsuspecting man show us how temptation works in our lives.

"I'M PURE."

"So she seizes him and kisses him, and with a brazen face she says to him: 'I was due to offer peace offerings; today I have paid my vows'" (vs. 13, 14 NASB).

The adulterous woman says, "See how pure I am? I've done my spiritual duties." When we first feel drawn toward something we shouldn't have but want, our immediate reaction is usually something like, "Oh, it's not that bad. God wouldn't want to deprive me of it."

We have two ways of determining whether or not something is sinful, even though our desires try to convince us it's not. The first is by studying the Bible. Many sinful things are mentioned: immorality, lying, stealing, murder, envy, homosexuality, bitterness, resentment, and unforgiveness. Additional attitudes and actions not mentioned in the Bible by name can also be sinful.

The second way to determine sin is if it draws us away

from a close relationship with God. Susannah Wesley said, "Whatever weakens your reason, impairs the tenderness of your conscience, obscures your sense of God, or takes away the relish of spiritual things; in short, whatever increases the strength and authority of your body over your mind—that thing is sin to you."[2]

James 4:17 adds, "Anyone, then, who knows the good he ought to do and doesn't do it, sins."

If you feel convicted about doing something and you do it anyway, you have sinned. We must also be careful to distinguish between real and false guilt.

Cindy was raised in a strict Christian home where playing cards and dancing were labeled sin. As an adult, she realized that an occasional game of cards and some forms of dancing were not necessarily sinful, but her childhood training caused deep guilt over them. In time, her "transformed mind" has been able to influence her emotions, and she can now play cards or dance without feeling guilty. Of course, Cindy isn't caught up in gambling or dancing every night, but when she plays a card game or square dances at a church social, she knows she doesn't have to condemn herself; she hasn't sinned.

Let me clarify, though, that habitual card playing or dancing in questionable places can be sin when accompanied by an attitude of indifference toward God. Many activities are or are not sinful depending on our attitude and God's plan for each of us.

My past struggle with sugar addiction is an example. For most people, eating sugar is not sinful, but for me it is. That doesn't mean I can't occasionally enjoy dessert or eat a piece of Christmas candy. It just means I have to prevent sugar from having the hold over me it did in the past.

When we know something is sin for us, we must

beware when we are tempted to believe, "It's not wrong for me."

"YOU ARE IMPORTANT."

"Therefore I have come out to meet you, to seek your presence earnestly, and I have found you" (Prov. 7:15, 16).

The adulteress tries to make her potential victim feel important. She pretends she was looking for him when in truth she was searching for any poor soul who strolled by.

Many times we are tempted: "Doing this will make me feel important." All of us have a valid need for significance; all of us need to feel important.

Larry Crabb writes,

People have one basic personal need which requires two kinds of input for its satisfaction. The most basic need is a sense of personal worth, an acceptance of oneself as a whole, real person. The two required inputs are *significance* (purpose, importance, adequacy for a job, meaningfulness, impact) and *security* (love—unconditional and consistently expressed; permanent acceptance).

I believe that before the Fall Adam and Eve were both significant and secure. From the moment of their creation their needs were fully met in a relationship with God unmarred by sin. Significance and security were attributes or qualities already resident within their personalities, so they never gave them a second thought. When sin ended their innocence and broke their relationship with God, what formerly were attributes now became needs.[3]

We can be tempted to meet this need for significance in wrong ways: working excessive hours to gain the approval of the boss while the needs of husband and children are ignored; giving in to bitterness because it concentrates on how we are hurt; saying yes to every request because we think something can't be done without us. We are tempted to try to falsely meet legitimate needs by believing such action will make us feel important.

"I'M ATTRACTIVE AND GOOD."

"I have spread my couch with coverings, with colored linens of Egypt. I have sprinkled my bed with myrrh, aloes and cinnamon" (Prov. 7:16, 17).

The adulterous woman makes her pleas sound irresistible. So it is when we are tempted. First John 2:16 describes temptation: "The cravings of sinful man, the lust of his eyes and the boasting of what he has and does." When we are tempted, we are lured with thoughts such as, "It will feel good," "It will taste good," "It can't be wrong when it seems so right."

Alexander MacLaren reminds us, "The temptation once yielded to gains power. The crack in the embankment which lets a drop or two ooze through is soon a hole which lets out a flood."[4]

When we think we can't resist flirting with an attractive man or taking a peek at a pornographic magazine, then for us the temptation becomes "coverings and colored linens."

"I'LL MEET YOUR NEEDS."

"Come, let us drink our fill of love until morning; Let us delight ourselves with caresses" (Prov. 7:18).

The temptress says, "I'll make you feel loved and satisfy your needs like you've never experienced before."

When we are tempted, our lust promises the same thing: permanent fulfillment and love. As a result, a single

Christian woman may accept her boyfriend's invitation to live with him or to engage in sexual activity. "I'll finally feel loved and accepted," she tells herself. A married Christian woman may be drawn into an affair because she believes another man will make her feel more loved than her husband does. But these incorrect ways of fulfilling the need for love and approval will end in disaster.

We must be quick to recognize our temptations for what they are: false ways to find fulfillment.

"NO ONE WILL EVER FIND OUT."

"For the man is not at home, he has gone on a long journey; he has taken a bag of money with him, at full moon he will come home" (Prov. 7:19, 20).

The adulterous woman tries to convince her victim that he is in no danger of discovery if he gives in to her lures. When we are tempted, we believe the same thing. "No one will find out, go ahead." "God won't do anything about it, it's okay."

But in our heart we know that every dark corner of our hearts will eventually be exposed, even if it's not until we reach heaven. Unfortunately, that knowledge isn't always strong enough to help us resist temptation's charms, and we end up paying the consequences. Hopefully, as women growing in security and God's strength, we can resist Satan's lie, "No one will ever find out." At that point we can reply, "Even if no one else finds out, God will know, and I want to please and obey him!"

TAKING AN INSIDE LOOK

All of us are tempted to believe that the desire that overwhelms us is pure, important, attractive, good, and will meet our needs. We also believe, "No one will ever find out." Something within each of us causes us to wrongfully give in to temptation.

Dr. Larry Crabb in his probing book, *Inside Out*, concludes that our unhealthy ways of dealing with the disappointments of life give fuel to our sinful longings. He writes,

> The power of bad habits is not simply in the pleasure they provide. Sinful habits become compulsively attractive when the pleasure they give relieves deep disappointment in the soul better than anything else one can imagine. The good feelings offered by having enjoyable sex, eating delicious food, or controlling crowds with skilled oratory can numb the ache of unmet longings by providing a satisfaction that, for a time, fulfills like nothing else ever has. People feel alive in the midst of consuming pleasure. Thus, whatever generates the pleasure seems so right. Pleasure of the body (such as sex or eating) and of the mind (such as power or applause) can be marvelous counterfeits of real life, when God has not been tasted. Their insidious appeal lies in their power to give quick relief from groaning, a relief that feels more than good—it feels like life.
>
> When pleasures of any kind are used to satisfy (or at least quiet) our crucial longings, then the craving for what only God can provide becomes a demanding tyrant, driving us toward whatever relief is available. Our god becomes our appetite. Crucial longings meant to create a panting after God energize our addiction to whatever feels good for a moment.[5]

Dr. Crabb tells about a young man who compulsively memorized scripture as a way to relieve the pain of his father's rejection. Then he explains,

It's clear that the purpose of the young man's obsession with Bible memorization was *not* to know God at any cost. His purpose was to relieve pain. Nothing is wrong, of course, with shaking the stone out of our shoe before continuing a walk. When relieving pain is not our final purpose in life, then it's reasonable to make ourself as comfortable as a responsible and moral approach to life permits. But when relief of the inevitable pain of living in a fallen world becomes our priority, at that moment we leave the path toward pursuing God. God's prescriptions for handling life do not relieve an ache that is not meant to cease this side of Heaven; they enable us to be faithful in the midst of it. Sometimes, the path of obedience even intensifies the pain in ways that seem entirely unfair, and even unkind of God.[6]

Crabb's comments remind me of what Jackie Barrile, the founder and president of Inner Development (ID), said to me. Jackie was delivered many years ago from severe bulimia, the binge-purge syndrome. After eating forty thousand calories of food in one binge, Jackie knelt before the Lord and prayed, "You're the only one who can help me, God. Please deliver me from bulimia."

Through sheer willpower Jackie didn't binge for the next seven days and believed God had healed her. On the eighth day, though, she binged worse than ever. She questioned God, "Lord, what went wrong? I came to you for help. What else can I do?"

Jackie says of that time, "In my spirit, God seemed to answer me: 'You turned to me for the wrong reason. Yes, I do have the power to deliver you, but that's not the reason I want you to come to me. I want you to get to know me better.' "

Tears flowing down her cheeks, Jackie knelt and prayed, "Lord, I'm sorry. You're right. Help me learn more about you." After that, even though she was still binging, the Bible became more important to her, and her relationship with God blossomed.

When Jackie sought God for the joy of knowing him, not for deliverance, her healing from bulimia began through a long process of finding the underlying causes of her eating disorder.

Jackie is an example of a woman growing in security and godliness. True godliness flows from an inner walk with God that is more than just "Do not handle! Do not taste! Do not touch!" (Col. 2:21). True godliness is to "set your hearts on things above, where Christ is seated at the right hand of God. Set your minds on things above, not earthly things. For you died, and your life is now hidden with Christ in God" (Col. 3:2, 3).

Seeking God for the sake of getting to know him better is the hallmark of a secure, godly woman. This is an ideal we want to move toward, but one which is difficult to attain.

I have far to go to reach that goal. Right now Darcy and Mark are happy children without any drastic crises to make life uncomfortable. But then I think, *Larry and I haven't been praying for them lately. We better start again so God won't make them disobey to make us seek him.*

Can you spot the inaccuracy in my thinking? The idea that I should seek God so that life will continue to go smoothly is false. Yes, I should seek God, but because I want to know him better and enjoy his fellowship—not because I want painless circumstances. As an imperfect person, my motive will most likely consist of both, but I can *choose* to desire to know God better.

The litmus test as to whether or not I'm growing in

godliness and security will come when my circumstances grow difficult (which will happen eventually because that is part of life). Will I then demand that God restore my comfort, or will I continue to seek him because I want to know him better—in the midst of pain and discomfort?

Godliness and security are intimately interrelated. When I'm secure in God's ability regardless of how crazy my world becomes, I can go through the fire with confidence and trust in God intact. In contrast, when I'm not secure in God, life's difficulties become overwhelming, and I'm forced to use my own manipulations to make life palatable again.

Few of us live in complete godliness and security. The majority of us are somewhere in between. To grow in these areas, we must take a look inside ourselves. When you do, what do you see? Do you see disappointments that seem easier to push back into your unconscious mind than to face? Do you remember hurt that hasn't been dealt with? Do you think, *Oh, that situation wasn't really that bad.* Or *They didn't understand what they were saying or doing. I've forgiven them.*

Yes, we do want to forgive, but true forgiveness comes when we fully experience our feelings from that incident, and then see how God was with us even then.

Be honest with yourself, and face the emotions stemming from hurts and disappointments. Maybe it will take inner healing with the guidance of a counselor or talking about it fully with a friend before healing can take place.

Larry Crabb says that we have two options. He writes,

We're left with the choice to run from the ache and wrap ourself in self-protection or to embrace the ache and rest secure in our Lord's promise: "Do not let your hearts be troubled . . . If I go and prepare a place for you, I will come back and take you to be with me that you also may be where I am" (John 14:1, 3). Self protection or trust: Every behavior ultimately reflects one choice or the other. We either accept groaning as a way of life and eagerly await our Lord's return with single-minded devotion to him, or we try to escape the unpleasantness of a groaning heart by denying the impact of any troubling reminder that life is not as it should be.[7]

We want to be that strong tree with deep roots in Jesus making the choice toward single-minded devotion to God. Psalm 101 gives us further guidelines for doing this.

KNOWING GOD

"I will sing of your love and justice; to you, O Lord, I will sing praise" (Ps. 101:1).

The first ingredient of a godly life is to know God. In this psalm, King David acknowledges the Almighty God as his Lord. God is the center of his life. As a result, he knows God intimately and communicates with him through prayer and praise.

You may be reading this book and have never made a commitment to Christ by asking him to forgive your sins. For many years, I considered myself a Christian because I was born in a "Christian" nation and attended church faithfully. It wasn't until I watched a Billy Graham film, "For Pete's Sake," and heard the gospel clearly presented that I understood I needed to ask Jesus to become the center of my life. I did this by confessing my sin, asking Jesus to cleanse me, and then determining to follow him.

If you've never asked Jesus to be your Savior and Lord, you can right now by praying: "Heavenly Father, I realize now I've made wrong choices that have separated me from you. I understand I can't save myself through good works but only by depending on Jesus who died in my place on the cross. I ask you to forgive me and cleanse me. Please be my Lord and Savior. Thank you for loving me. Because of your faithfulness I know you've heard me and made me a new creature in Christ. I ask these things in Jesus' name. Amen."

If you sincerely prayed this prayer, you are a Christian! I welcome you to the family of God and encourage you to tell another Christian about your decision so that you may learn more about what it means to be a child of God. Just like David, God is now your Lord and you've laid the foundation for a godly walk.

DESIRING A SANCTIFIED LIFE

"I will be careful to lead a blameless life—when will you come to me? I will walk in my house with a blameless heart" (Ps. 101:2).

Sanctification means *setting apart*. Therefore, like David, the secure, godly woman is careful to lead a blameless life and "walk in [her] house with a blameless heart." The secure woman knows she is set apart from sin in God's eyes (her perfect position in Christ) and is growing closer to Jesus (her imperfect performance on this earth).

Sanctification begins with choices. David said "I will" twice in this verse. He makes these choices with his will, not his feelings, hand-in-hand with the empowering of the Holy Spirit.

This concept reminds me of a scene I saw in a park. A young couple and their three-year-old son were training their German Shepherd puppy. The husband and wife stood about fifty feet apart, and the husband called the dog, "Lucky, come!" while bringing his arm toward his chest. Lucky bounded over to the man and was rewarded with petting. Then the wife did the same thing, and Lucky ran to her.

The little boy joined them. He called to the dog and awkwardly tried to imitate the motions his parents had made. Lucky stared at the boy, took a few steps, and sat down. The boy called again but Lucky hesitated.

Then, without the boy's realizing it, the father silently moved behind him and motioned with his arm as the boy called, "Lucky, come!" Lucky immediately ran toward the child on his way to the father. The little boy jumped up and down with delight, hugging the dog, believing Lucky had obeyed his commands.

It's the same as we live the sanctified life. We make the right motions (do the right things), and good happens but not because of us. Rather, because God is within us strengthening us to resist sin, giving us faith to believe his word, and empowering us to minister in his name. We may feel *we* have the power, but all the while, the Spirit is really the one who brings the results. And yes, we'll still make right choices, but that's also because of his indwelling presence and power within us.

We may not always feel or know for sure that God is leading us, but living by faith means believing God is commanding areas of struggle to submit to him.

EVALUATING INFLUENCES

"I will set before my eyes no vile thing" (Ps. 101:3).

Here David makes a godly choice to be selective in what influences him. Second Corinthians 10:5 tells us as godly women to "take captive every thought to make it obedient to Christ." We must screen our thinking to filter out anything that can draw us away from Christ.

George Sweeting says, "When my gasoline tank registers empty, I know it is full—that is, it is full of air. But the automobile was not built to run on air. To displace the air, I must fill it with gasoline. God's cure to evil thinking is to fill our minds with that which is good."[8]

When I became a Christian at age eighteen, my ears had an appetite for rock 'n' roll music. When I first tuned into a Christian radio station as I drove back and forth to college, my ears rebelled. I didn't like the tempo or the words. I could listen for only a few moments. But day after day, I made a choice to turn to that Christian station and listen to it as long as possible. Many months passed before my "appetite" appreciated those "spiritual sounds." Eventually they were all I wanted to listen to, except for an occasional side portion of oldies but goodies.

Replacing old nature hearing and thinking with new nature hearing and thinking will create a more godly life. What influences diminish your security in Christ? Does watching a movie whose plot is based on an extramarital affair make you anxious about your relationship with your husband? After the movie, do you find yourself nagging him about his away-from-home activities? Maybe your parents divorced when you were young, and you haven't faced the pain it brought. If your parents' marriage didn't survive, you wonder whether yours can.

Do you easily become depressed or bitter when someone disappoints you? Perhaps you were raised in an alcoholic home where your father failed to keep his promises. Identify where your depression comes from and work through it. You may want to attend an Adult Children of Alcoholics (ACOA) meeting.

I must guard against reading newspaper ads of clothes sales. Invariably the ads convince me that if I don't hurry, I've lost my last opportunity to buy. I know what I'm experiencing is a result of the lie I believed as a child—that my self-esteem and value were based on how I

Sure Footing in a Shaky World

dressed. As I skim through the ads now, I correct my wrong self-talk by telling myself, *I don't need to buy something just because it's on sale. There will be other sales. I'm not missing out.* Then my peace returns.

Each of us has a choice as to what our minds dwell on. Like David, we need to make sure our eyes and minds don't dwell on "vile thing(s)."

SEPARATING MYSELF FROM UNGODLINESS

"The deeds of faithless men I hate; they will not cling to me. Men of perverse heart shall be far from me; I will have nothing to do with evil. Whoever slanders his neighbor in secret, him will I put to silence; whoever has haughty eyes and proud heart, him will I not endure" (Ps. 101:3-5).

David separated himself from all people who might have an ungodly influence on him. He has already set himself apart from ungodly thinking; now he sets himself apart from ungodly people.

Although we all have contact with non-Christians, we must be careful not to be influenced by their ungodly principles or activities. Someone has said that "we must come out of the world, get the world out of us, then go back into the world." We can also determine whether a friendship pulls us away from our beliefs or tears down our self-esteem.

Sheila experienced this. Every time she talked to her grandmother, she felt defeated. Although she dearly loved this grandmother who had raised her, Sheila recognized the woman was highly critical and negative. Nothing Sheila did pleased or satisfied her.

After counseling with a friend about her struggle, Sheila decided not to phone her grandmother any more. When her grandmother phoned, she cut the conversation short as politely as possible. For a year, she held to her resolution until she felt in control of her life. As she grew stronger in the Lord, she eventually knew she could handle her grandmother's negativism on a limited scale. Whenever she felt the negativism seeping into her spirit, she politely ended the conversation. Now, two years later, Sheila is at peace with herself and strong enough to keep her focus on the Lord in spite of contact with her grandmother.

Like Sheila, the secure woman knows God doesn't want her to remove herself from the world, but she realizes she has a choice about who and what influences her.

SURROUNDING MYSELF WITH GODLY PEOPLE

"My eyes will be on the faithful in the land, that they may dwell with me; he whose walk is blameless will minister to me" (Ps. 101:6).

David aligns himself with people of God who will have a godly impact upon him. We do this when we don't "give up meeting together . . . but encourage one another" (Heb. 10:25). Getting involved in a church where other Christians will hold us accountable is a primary ingredient in a godly woman's life. A small group Bible study or women's fellowship group is also important. Staying strong in our commitment to Christ is easier if we are surrounded and encouraged by those who love the same things we do. We'll also want to form deep friendships with other Christian women.

For those who refuse to get involved in a church because of "those hypocrites there," let me say that church was never intended for perfect people. If we were perfect, we wouldn't need a church. Instead, we meet together as Christians because we need each other and because God commands it.

REPRESENTING CHRIST TO UNBELIEVERS

"No one who practices deceit will dwell in my house; no one who speaks falsely will stand in my presence. Every morning I will put to silence all the wicked in the land; I will cut off every evildoer from the city of the Lord" (Ps. 101:7, 8).

As king, David had the power to do many things that we don't. Instead, God wants us to represent him by speaking to unbelievers of his love and salvation.

Although we are not to be influenced toward evil by those who don't know God, we must still have contact with them to tell them of God's salvation plan. Whether by brief encounters with people we meet each day or by developing friendships, we are told by God to "go and make disciples of all nations, baptizing them in the name of the Father and of the Son and of the Holy Spirit, and teaching them to obey everything I commanded you. And surely I am with you always, to the very end of the age" (Matt. 28:19, 20). In the next chapter, we'll look at some practical ways to do this.

The other day when the high winds uprooted my neighbor's tree, many other trees continued to stand strong and deeply rooted. To me those healthy trees represent secure women who remain strong in their godly walk with Christ regardless of the winds of temptation that blow through their branches.

With which group would you like to identify yourself? The fact that you've read this far speaks of your intention to grow deeply rooted in Christ, standing strong in him. The Holy Spirit will do this within you. As the tree described in Psalm 1:3, you "will be like a tree firmly planted by streams of water, which yields its fruit in its season, and its leaf does not wither; and in whatever [you]

166

do, [you] prosper" (NASB).

Can't you see yourself standing like that tree? Secure, nourished by God's love, fruitful in the gifts of the Spirit, in bringing others to Christ?

As you continue to resist temptation and make godly choices, secure in God's love, this can be true.

11

· · ·

A Secure Woman Boldly Shares Her Faith

I'm not very secure in my ability to share my faith. Even though I've had occasional successes and led several people to Christ, this is an area I continue to grow in. The reasons for my insecurity are several. See if you identify with any of them.

I'm insecure about witnessing because I'm afraid of rejection. None of us likes rejection. Our natural instinct is to avoid it at all costs.

Yet, when I face my fears of being rejected, I must acknowledge that any rejection I've received in the past isn't that bad. I've never been spit on, hit, yelled at, or otherwise mistreated. I'm afraid of the more subtle things people can do: raise an eyebrow to indicate they think I'm a bit weird; smile lazily as if to let me know they couldn't care less; or listen patiently, even though they have no intention of doing anything about the gospel.

What are your fears? When you analyze them, are they as bad as you expected? Will sharing your faith result in a beating, imprisonment, or death?

Sometimes I face the fact that such penalties could actually lessen our fears and give us more courage. Christians in Communist countries suffer greatly for sharing their faith, while the worst that will happen to me is a raised eyebrow. Persecution strengthens our faith in God's strength.

When we witness and sense rejection, we should remember that it is *Jesus* the person is rejecting—not us if we're representing Christ in a loving way. If we're obnoxious in our sharing or insensitive to the needs of that person, then, of course, we must change our tactics.

But if we're loving and people still don't respond to our sharing, it may be for several reasons:

• they aren't yet aware of their need for salvation;

• they are misinformed about what the Bible says or who Jesus is;

• they are concerned more about the cares of this world than their eternal destiny;

• they are deliberately rejecting Jesus even though they feel God's drawing in their life.

When we understand that the fault may not be ours, we can accept where the other person is and continue to pray for him and other opportunities to share.

As we plan to talk to someone about Jesus, we'll have more courage if we think positively. Maybe he'll be thrilled to hear about God's love for him. This happened to me.

Several years ago, I felt God's nudge to visit my new neighbor across the street. I asked God what he wanted me to tell her, and he seemed to reply, "That I love her."

Fighting back my fears of appearing silly, I imagined her being very receptive to God's words.

Fearfully, I crossed the street and knocked on her door. When she answered, I gulped and said, "God wants me to tell you he loves you."

She looked at me in surprise. "My son and I were just talking about that," she said. "Come on in." Over the next several weeks we studied the Bible together, and in time, she received Christ. My expectation of a positive response gave me the courage I needed to see good fruit produced.

I'm insecure about witnessing because I'm afraid of failure. If the unbeliever I'm talking to doesn't respond with a decision for Christ, won't that mean I'm a failure?

No. The results of my sharing and the response of the unbeliever are not my responsibility. My only responsibility is to obey God and do what he tells me to do.

"Our immediate concern is not to extract agreement or to win arguments; it is to produce understanding," Jim Petersen writes in *Evangelism for Our Generation.* "We need to leave room for disagreement and doubt. It is the Holy Spirit alone who convicts of sin, righteousness, and judgment, not us. It is the Bible that reveals the true intents of the heart. We should leave these responsibilities where they belong. Our part as we co-labor with God is to bring the non-Christian into contact with these powers, and to love him as he struggles his way out of his rebellion and into faith."[1]

Our definition of evangelism can contribute to this feeling of failure. If we think of evangelism only as getting the person to receive Christ, most of our interaction with unbelievers will be judged failures. But if we regard evangelism as encouraging a person to take one step closer to a personal acceptance of Jesus, then we can often consider our dialogue successful.

"Rather than looking for a single step, it is better to think in terms of mini-decisions. If evangelism is a process, then our function is to accompany our acquaintances down the road to Christ, showing them the way. We must walk the road with them, a step at a time."[2]

The next time you feel insecure about witnessing, determine if you're thinking in terms of, *What if he/she doesn't receive Christ?* If so, you can tell yourself, *That isn't my responsibility. I'll just help him/her consider what the Bible says.*

I'm insecure about witnessing because I feel inadequate. "What will I say? How can I explain my own struggles? What if they ask questions I can't answer?"

I'm amazed that Jesus gave the responsibility of representing him to humans, especially imperfect people like Peter, who easily overreacted; Thomas, whose faith was based on sight; Paul, who had physical problems; and Timothy, who was young and inexperienced. Can you identify with one of them? If you can, you know that if you'd lived in Jesus time, he would have been glad to have you as his witness. Joseph Bayly writes, "Jesus Christ didn't commit the gospel to an advertising agency; He commissioned disciples."[3]

We may think that non-Christians are looking for perfect representatives of the Christian life; actually, they are usually turned off by such people because they don't seem "real." They're actually looking for Christians who have similar struggles and yet have found answers or are in the process of finding them. Consequently, if someone asks you a question you can't answer, just say, "I don't know the answer to your question, but I'll try to find out and get back to you."

We can also relax when we realize we don't have to clear up every misunderstanding or explain the "inconsistencies" in the Bible. Sometimes we can only say, "To tell you the truth, this is an area that even theologians don't agree on. I'm confident there's an explanation, but I just don't know it, and at this point, no one else is sure either."

An effective way to communicate God's truths is to engage non-Christian friends in a Bible study and then ask questions as you go along. We don't always have to be the "answer-man" in the study. It's all right for people to express their doubts. Yet often we become insecure in the face of questions or doubts.

Jim Petersen explains,

How we react to these questions will affect the level of communication between us from then on. If we respond with dogmatism (which is a form of insecurity) or with defensiveness (which is another form of insecurity), the non-Christian will quickly understand the rules of the game and will proceed accordingly. He will either operate within our limitations— or he will disappear. But if we demonstrate an attitude that encourages the expression of doubts and questions, our effectiveness will be far greater.[4]

Many times, as I've led a Bible study, I've sensed insecurity rise within me. Perhaps someone expresses their shock at all the killing by the Israelites in the Old Testament, and I begin to feel tense. I want to defend what happened because I don't want them to think inaccurately of God.

But God doesn't need me to defend him. I don't have to take someone's comments personally. I can calmly state why I think such things happened and leave the results of how the other person receives it to the Lord. God hasn't hired me to be his lawyer, but I can be his witness.

I'm insecure about witnessing because I don't know how to do it. Later in this chapter, we'll talk about some techniques, but right now, we can be assured that one way or another, we're already doing "it." Each one of us is a witness if we're a Christian. Our lives and the choices we make are testimonies—attractive or not—of our relationship with God.

Emmanuel Suhard says, "To be a witness does not consist of engaging in propaganda or in stirring people up. It means to live in such a way that one's life would not make sense if God did not exist."[5]

We may also lack boldness in sharing Christ because we think in terms of telling the other person what to do. We think we must convince her. Changing our goal from "telling" to "guiding" will give us more confidence.

"Instead of telling people what they need to do, we want to bring them into an understanding of who Jesus is," says Jim Petersen. "As this understanding grows, the response—what the person needs to do—becomes self-evident. I have found that, more often than not, when the truth about Christ is fully understood, the response occurs without my help."[6]

I'm insecure about witnessing because I compare myself to others. "I can't be an effective witness because I'm not bubbly like Sylvia." "I don't know as much about the Bible as Julia, so I better not say anything."

Comparing ourselves to other Christians is a fast way to grow insecure in our own strengths and abilities. Instead, if we'll understand what I call the four different witnessing styles, we'll be able to accept ourselves the way God made us and use our strengths to be bold witnessers.

THE VIVACIOUS WITNESS

Jenny, a vivacious witness, is spirited, fun-loving, talkative, and can easily bring her faith into the conversation. Enthusiastically, she tells what Christ has done for her. Alert to any new opportunity, she loves sharing about Jesus.

The vivacious witnessing style is usually the style most of us unfavorably compare our own with. Yet, just as no one is perfect, the vivacious person has weaknesses also. When a friend expresses a need, people like Jenny quickly tell her they'll pray about it, but then frequently forget their promise.

In fact, Jenny is often forgetful and unorganized in following through on the contacts she makes for Christ. For instance, she may invite a person to church but then forget to call to finalize the plans. When she leads a person to Christ, her busy schedule gets in the way of discipling that person into a mature Christian.

People love to be with Jenny because of her enthusiasm and light-hearted outlook on life, but being an attentive listener is not one of her strong points; she talks too much. Finally, when she shares the gospel, she sometimes makes it sound too easy and rosy, as if becoming a Christian will solve all of a person's problems.

A vivacious witness such as Jenny can grow into an effective representative of Christ as she learns to depend on the Holy Spirit for strength to listen to others and to follow through.

THE SHY WITNESS

Alicia is a basically peaceful person, and as a result, her personal witnessing style is the one I call shy. Never one to express her opinions, when it comes to sharing Christ people like Alicia often feel inadequate. Their main concerns are wanting people to feel comfortable and wondering whether others will still like them if they mention

Jesus. Out of their feelings of inadequacy comes a fear that their testimony isn't interesting enough to share.

Because Alicia is naturally quiet, she is a good listener. Once she becomes more confident at witnessing, aided by some effective witnessing tools, she can use that listening ability to full advantage. Because she doesn't say anything unless it's important, people usually listen and respect her when she does express an opinion about her faith in Jesus.

Alicia also has difficulty being motivated because she doesn't recognize the mission field around her. But when people point out the needs of others, she can be a sensitive, caring ambassador for Christ.

With instruction and more self-confidence, Alicia can become a powerful soul winner.

THE SERIOUS WITNESS

I'm an example of the serious witness. For example, I had been praying for my neighbor, Sue, for several months. I'd invited her to evangelistic events and shared my testimony with her. When I asked her if she'd ever made Jesus her Savior, she told me she had when she was thirteen. I rejoiced, but as time went on, she didn't seem interested in spiritual things, such as the Bible study I invited her to attend. I didn't know how to proceed.

A year or so later, Sue experienced some traumatic events in her life, including the death of her father. As we talked one day, she seemed open to talk about spiritual issues. It dawned on me that I could challenge her to make Christ her Savior and Lord. When I asked her, "Are you saying you want to ask Jesus to be your Savior?" she replied, "Yes, I don't really think I did before. I want to do it now."

Sue repeated the sinner's prayer after me. Both of us

cried as we happily hugged each other. She had finally found what she was looking for, and I was so glad I hadn't given up praying for her and looking for opportunities to speak of God's love.

As a serious witness, I frequently find witnessing hard work. Since I am a perfectionist, I want all the elements of presenting Christ to be exactly right before I dive in. If I only have a few minutes with a person, I tell myself there isn't enough time. If a friend doesn't seem to show interest in spiritual things, I convince myself it's useless to try. If there's the slightest possibility a person won't respond positively, I won't risk rejection.

I will rise to the occasion, though, when I'm challenged to witness for Christ. If my Bible study leader suggests I give my testimony to one person that week, I will perform, even if it means dumping my testimony on any person who comes along.

However cautious a serious witness may be, she usually has a sensitivity to people's needs and hurts that can make her "ought to" witnessing effective.

The greatest strength we serious representatives of Christ have is our dependability. When we invite someone to a Bible study or woman's meeting at church, we make sure we do everything possible to help that person come. And when we lead a person to Christ, we'll begin a Bible study with her or see that she gets plugged into some discipleship group.

When the serious witness concentrates on relaxing in the Holy Spirit's power and gives up her perfectionist thinking, she can be a dynamic witness for Christ.

THE CONTROLLING WITNESS

Valerie represents the controlling witnessing style. As a spokesperson for Christ, she struggles in her tendency to force people to do what she thinks is best for them. Therefore, she can lack sensitivity and find it hard to be a good listener. She doesn't want to discuss at length why a person should become a Christian, she just wants them to do it. In Valerie's mind, there's no need for explanations because it's so obvious that Christ is the solution for their problems.

At the same time, Valerie can be effective because she isn't concerned about what other people think of her. She has the confidence to know Jesus is the answer and will share that secret with power. However, when a person comes to know Christ, she may tell her everything she needs to do, rather than encourage her to find out what the Bible says she should do.

When she allows the Holy Spirit to express his compassion through her, Valerie can be a sensitive witness for Jesus.

As you see, no witnessing style is perfect; each one has strengths and weaknesses. And we may even be a combination of witnessing styles. Consequently, we as well can stop trying to compare our style to another's, thinking we can't represent Christ unless we change. When we do, we can be more secure in witnessing. God wants us to operate within the strength of our individual style and allow him to diminish our weaknesses.

Although he can help us change, we'll most likely continue to operate within our basic style for the most part. God can use every one of us; he has a place and purpose for each person. Instead of feeling inferior because we don't act like another witness, let's ask God how he wants to develop our particular style into a bold witness for him. However he leads us to reach out to others, knowing our own personal witnessing style will help us use our strengths and diminish our weaknesses.

Let's now look at some tools we can use to become the bold witnesses God wants us to be.

OUR LIFESTYLE

All witnessing stems from our lifestyle: the choices we make and the lives we lead. As I said before, whether or not we're aware of it, we witness by the way we live.

In our insecurity, this fact sometimes causes us to wear masks. We don't want to be vulnerable for fear non-Christians will think God doesn't have the answers.

The secure woman learns that sharing her problems with unbelievers is the right thing to do. Talking about how God is helping her in the midst of difficulties gives her credibility and develops the faith of her non-Christian friend.

The next time you think, "Well, I'm not a witness for Jesus, I haven't talked to anyone about him today," remember your very life is a witness for him.

All of our Christian life needs a foundation of prayer, and witnessing for Christ is no different. Whether we start out the day dedicating ourselves to being sensitive to the needs of others or sending up arrow prayers at appropriate moments, we need the Holy Spirit's direction and power. Asking God to give us his loving concern for others can begin the process of changing from an "ought to" to a "want to" witness.

ASKING QUESTIONS AND LISTENING

One of our main goals in witnessing should be to find out how God is already working in the other person's life. We can ask her questions:

"Tell me about your relationship with God."

"Do you ever think about God?"

"Do you realize you can know God personally?"

"Do you know Jesus loves you?"

"What does Christmas (or Easter) mean to you?"

"Did you know you can be assured of going to heaven?"

"Did you know you can have your sins forgiven?"

"What's your church background?"

"What's your secret of happiness?"

Asking these or similar questions opens the door to further conversation about spiritual issues.

TELLING YOUR OWN STORY

One of the most effective tools any of us has is the story of how we came to know Christ. Even if we're a brand-new Christian and haven't learned any Bible verses or principles, we can tell someone else how we met Christ. Because it's our own experience, no one can deny it happened to you.

People love to hear other's experiences, and your story will hold their attention. I have my "testimony" boiled down to four minutes, and I've never had anyone object to my telling them a four-minute story.

Here's a basic outline your story could follow:

A. What your life was like before meeting Christ: where you grew up; your family and church background; your traumas and struggles; your understanding of Christ at that time.

B. How you came to know Christ: who told you the gospel; your initial reaction; what the Bible says about salvation; a Bible verse that was particularly meaningful or helpful to you; the brief prayer you prayed; your final reaction.

C. What your life is like now, living with Christ: how Jesus has helped you; a verse that has become special; what areas the Lord is working on in your life presently.

D. What you can ask the other person to encourage her

to consider the claims of Christ: "Have you had a similar experience to mine?" "Have you ever wondered how you can know God personally?" "Has anyone ever told you a story like mine?"

Write down your testimony and practice it. Of course, as the Holy Spirit prompts you to share with others, you'll want to be flexible.

SHARE A SCRIPTURAL TRUTH

When sharing scriptural truths, include one verse you've memorized or the whole gospel message of:
- Jesus is God.
- Jesus died for my sins.
- Jesus rose from the grave and is alive today. Because of his sacrifice, I can live eternally.
- I must acknowledge Christ died for me personally and submit my life to him.

If you don't have a lot of time or there's no opportunity to befriend the person, a quick scriptural truth can plant a seed or water an already-planted seed.

If someone shares a pleasant experience with you, you can say, "God sure gives us some good gifts, doesn't he?" Or if an acquaintance laments over the struggles in her life, you can respond, "It's good to know God loves us even during the hard times."

USING CHRISTIAN BOOKS AND TRACTS

My friend, Mary Ann Mooney, is a prime example of a person who uses tracts effectively. One day when she was in an elevator, a man quickly jumped in just as the door was closing. "Whew, you have to make *quick* decisions in this life or get left behind," he said.

Mary Ann's spiritual ears perked up at this, and she answered, "Yes, you certainly do, don't you? I'm not going to be left behind when Jesus comes back, are you?"

She offered him a booklet she had with her. She had aroused the man's curiosity, and he promised to read it.

Just recently, Mary Ann visited a sick friend at a local hospital. As she got in the elevator, a man joined her and with a smile said, "Are you going up?"

Mary Ann knew he was joking since they were on the top floor but she answered, "Yes, as a matter of fact I am. I'm going up to heaven some day, are you?"

The man was a bit surprised and explained, "Oh, I meant it as a joke."

With a twinkle in her eye, Mary Ann replied, "Well, I was very serious. Would you like to read a booklet that tells you how to know whether you're going to heaven?"

The man gladly accepted the booklet she handed him, and they said goodbye when they reached the bottom floor.

Mary Ann can tell of many such incidents when she has been alert to God's leading and given out a tract or shared the gospel message. She never goes anywhere without her supply of tracts.

Giving gospel tracts to a person or leaving them in waiting rooms, airplanes, restrooms, and businesses is something any of us can do.

If the person is open at all, it's a good idea to spend a minute or two going through the booklet or tract with him. Otherwise, he may not read it.

Christian books are another tool that can be given to unbelievers as gifts—for birthdays, anniversaries, baby showers, weddings, or other occasions. Many good books, which aren't too heavy on the spiritual side yet clearly present Christ as the answer, are available.

We won't always see the seeds that we plant grow in Christian lives, but we can believe that God will bring other people to water and to reap. At other times, we'll be able to follow through and involve the person in a Bible study or church fellowship.

Growing in boldness to be secure representatives of Jesus is an on-going process. As we continue to seek the Lord as to how he wants us to live and speak of him, he will be faithful to show us.

Epilogue
. . .
Our Security Depends on God

We've come a long way in our journey toward greater security. We've looked at our position in Christ, the power of prayer, coping with problems, and being protected against opposition. We've talked about confronting sin, and we've examined our life assumptions. Perseverance and failure, along with godly living and witnessing, have also kept our minds busy. We won't be able to immediately put all these ideas into practice, but we'll work on them over time, allowing the Lord to fashion us into more secure women.

As this happens, our foundation for security will be based on the character of God. "The [women] who know their God will display strength and take action" (Dan. 11:32). What a beautiful description of a secure woman:

one who has a balance of strength and action, her security dependent on her knowledge of God.

I hope these closing thoughts on God's character deepen your feelings of security:

• Because God is loving, he'll choose only the best for me. Therefore, I can be secure.

• Because God is dependable, he'll keep all his promises. Therefore, I can be secure.

• Because God is holy, he'll faithfully mold me closer to his Son's image. Therefore, I can be secure.

• Because God is patient, he'll require no more from me than is reasonable for my faith. Therefore, I can be secure.

• Because God is sovereign, he'll control my comings and goings. Therefore, I can be secure.

• Because God is forgiving, he'll always pardon my sins. Therefore, I can be secure.

• Because God is stable, he'll never change. Therefore, I can be secure.

• Because God is wise, he'll give me insights and understanding. Therefore, I can be secure.

• Because God is creative, he'll provide solutions that are beyond my imagination. Therefore, I can be secure.

• Because God is available, he'll always be watching for my attention. Therefore, I can be secure.

Keep your eyes on him. His eye is on you, princess of the King.

Source Notes

CHAPTER 1

1. Larry Crabb, *Effective Biblical Counseling* (Grand Rapids: Zondervan, 1977), pp. 61, 62.
2. Crabb, *Effective Biblical Counseling*, pp. 70, 71.
3. Crabb, *Effective Biblical Counseling*, p. 69.

CHAPTER 2

1. George Sweeting, *Great Quotes and Illustrations* (Waco, TX: Word, 1985), p. 204.
2. Augustus Strong, *Systematic Theology* (Valley Forge, PA: Judson Press), pp. 287, 288.
3. Evelyn Christenson, *What Happens When Women Pray* (Wheaton: Victor, 1975), p. 67.

4. Ray Stedman, *Spiritual Warfare* (Portland, OR: Multnomah, 1975), pp. 136, 137.

5. Christenson, p. 15.

6. Catherine Marshall, *Adventures in Prayer* (Old Tappan, NJ: Chosen Books, 1975), p. 14.

CHAPTER 3

1. Dr. M. Scott Peck, *The Road Less Traveled* (New York: Touchstone Books, Simon and Schuster, 1978), p. 16.

2. Paul Lee Tan, *Encyclopedia of 7700 Illustrations*, (Rockville, MD: Assurance Publishers, 1979), p. 1509.

3. Tan, p. 1509.

4. Peck, p. 29.

5. Warren and Ruth Myers, quoted in *Discovering God's Will* (Colorado Springs: NavPress, 1980), p. 89.

6. Myers, p. 57.

7. Myers, p. 57.

8. Christenson, p. 66.

CHAPTER 4

1. David D. Burns, "Aim For Success, Not Perfection," *Readers Digest,* March 1985, p. 72.

2. Wayne Coffey, "Is It Worth It To Be Perfect?" *Seventeen*, November 1984, p. 183.

3. Sandra Simpson LeSourd, *The Compulsive Woman* (Old Tappan, NJ: Chosen Books, 1987), pp. 252, 253.

4. LeSourd, pp. 252, 253.

CHAPTER 5

1. Melody Beattie, *Codependent No More* (New York: Harper/Hazelden Books, 1987), p. 31.

2. Beattie, p. 2.
3. LeSourd, p. 262.
4. Beattie, p. 211.
5. Beattie, p. 214.

CHAPTER 6

1. Alan Redpath, *Victorious Christian Service* (Old Tappan, NJ: Revell, 1958), pp. 110, 111.

2. Ranald Macauley and Jerram Barrs, *Christianity with a Human Face* (Downers Grove, IL: Intervarsity Press, 1978), p. 96.

3. Joyce Huggett, *Creative Conflict* (Downers Grove, IL: Intervarsity Press, 1984), p. 20.

4. David Augsburger, *Caring Enough to Confront* (Ventura, CA: Regal, 1973), p. 47.

5. Maurice Wagner, *Put It All Together* (Grand Rapids: Zondervan, 1974), p. 99.

6. Huggett, p. 84.
7. Wagner, p. 26.
8. Los Angeles Times, December 27, 1988.

CHAPTER 7

1. Crabb, *Effective Biblical Counseling*, p. 78.
2. Crabb, *Effective Biblical Counseling*, p. 140.

CHAPTER 8

1. Jean Huff Graham, "Escaping Burnout," *Virtue*, September 1986, pp. 14, 15.

2. "Escaping Burnout," pp. 14, 15.

3. Joseph M. Stowell, "Bigger Picture People," *Moody Monthly*, October 1987, p. 30.

4. Quoted in an article by Pat King, "Why Is Saying No So Hard?" *Virtue*, September 1986, p. 16.

5. Pat King, "Nine Ways to Say No," *Virtue*, September 1986, p. 18. Taken from *How to Have All the Energy You Need Every Day* (Wheaton: Tyndale House, 1986).

6. Tan, p. 1139.

7. Anonymous.

CHAPTER 9

1. Sweeting, p. 109.

2. Sherwood Eliot Wirt and Kersten Beckstrom, *Topical Encyclopedia of Living Quotations* (Minneapolis: Bethany House Publishers, 1982), p. 74.

3. Augsburger, p. 109.

4. Charles G. Ward, "I'm a Christian—Why Do I Keep Sinning?" *Decision*, May 1987, pp. 1-8.

5. Jill Briscoe, *Today's Christian Woman*, July/August 1987, p. 50.

6. Briscoe, *Today's Christian Woman,* p. 50.

CHAPTER 10

1. Sweeting, p. 246.

2. Wirt and Beckstrom, p. 227.

3. Crabb, *Effective Biblical Counseling*, p. 61.

4. Sweeting, p. 246.

5. Larry Crabb, *Inside Out* (Colorado Springs: Nav-Press, 1988), pp. 96, 97.

6. Crabb, *Inside Out*, pp. 73, 74.

7. Crabb, *Inside Out*, p. 99.

8. Sweeting, p. 247.

CHAPTER 11

1. Jim Petersen, *Evangelism for Our Generation* (Colorado Springs: NavPress, 1985), p. 115.
2. Petersen, p. 97.
3. Sweeting, p. 261.
4. Petersen, p. 125
5. Wirt and Beckstrom, p. 256.
6. Petersen, p. 55.

Inquiries regarding speaking availability and other correspondence may be directed to Kathy Collard Miller at the following address:

P.O. Box 1058
Placentia, CA 92670